AQUAMARINE BLUE 5

AQUAMARINE BLUE 5

Personal Stories

of College Students

with Autism

EDITED BY DAWN PRINCE-HUGHES

SWALLOW PRESS / OHIO UNIVERSITY PRESS / ATHENS

Swallow Press/Ohio University Press, Athens, Ohio 45701
© 2002 by Dawn Prince-Hughes
Printed in the United States of America
All rights reserved

Swallow Press/Ohio University Press books are printed on acid-free
paper ⊚ ™

10 09 08 07 06 05 04 03 02   5 4 3 2 1

Library of Congress Cataloging-in-Publication Data
Aquamarine blue 5 : personal stories of college students with autism /
    edited by Dawn Prince-Hughes.
        p. cm.
    Includes bibliographical references.
    ISBN 0-8040-1053-6 (cloth : alk. paper) — ISBN 0-8040-1054-4 (pbk. :
alk. paper)
    1. Autistic youth—Education. 2. College students with disabilities—
Attitudes. 3. College students' writings. I. Title: Aquamarine blue
five. II. Prince-Hughes, Dawn, 1964–

LC4717.5. A7 2002
371.94—dc21

                                                            2002075508

For my parents, who came before me,

and Aris, who came after.

Contents

> *Garry writes about the loneliness and isolation people with autism can face as they try to navigate the university system. His essay also speaks to the durability of human will and the ways that small successes can lead to larger ones.*

> *Guiding us through a variety of personal examples of his difficulties and successes, Darius argues strongly for the importance of diversity both within the university and throughout the world as a whole.*

> *In her essay, Michelle talks specifically about her odd eating habits, a characteristic shared by many ASD people. Her writings remind us that autistic features are likely to show up in unexpected places—in this case, the school cafeteria—and that misdiagnosis of ASD can stretch as far as Anorexia Nervosa.*

> *In reminding us that "spiritual autism" is far worse than physical autism, Crocus also helps those in the university system remember that students are complex weavings of both body and spirit.*

Preface

As an anthropologist and research scientist at a university, I have become interested in the emerging "autistic culture." The initial reasons for my interest are obvious: autistic culture is new and dynamic, it is in an initial phase of growth, and it comprises people who do not easily form relationships. Unlike "deaf culture" or "blind culture," autistic culture has only become possible in the age of the Internet. The Internet and its many chat groups and listservs dedicated to people diagnosed with an Autism Spectrum Disorder (ASD) have encouraged the rapid growth of a thriving community.

Why because of the Internet? Firstly because several symptoms of autism, such as difficulty coping in social situations, aversion to direct eye contact, and difficulty quickly responding conversationally, prevent many people with autism from finding each other and organizing sustainable real-time meetings (I hasten to add that this is not always the case).

Secondly because people with ASD are scattered physically, so that simple logistics prevents large communities of people with autism from meeting.

In addition to my interest as an anthropologist, my membership in the university community and an awareness of our need in that community to learn about diversity has informed this process. As a writer, also, I have found the project of great interest. Autistic autobiography is rare and therefore, in my opinion, valuable.

However, it is as an autistic person myself that I am chiefly invested in this anthology.

Francesca Happé has claimed, in her essay "The Autobiographical Writings of Three Asperger Syndrome Adults: Problems of Interpretation and Implications for Theory,"[1] that the most coherent, most relevant and revealing autobiographies of people on the autistic spectrum are of dubious value as they are, by necessity, edited with a heavy hand —even translated, if you will—by "normal" people who end up making the work mostly their own. She has charged that both professionals and the community at large will always have a hard time learning anything substantial from autobiographical works for this reason; they will be incomprehensible if they are left untouched, but worthless if edited.

I am in substantial disagreement with Ms. Happé. I have become familiar with certain patterns as I transcribed these essays (it was validating to see the patterns were similar to the ones I have struggled with as a professional writer). I believe these patterns are important for what they reveal in themselves. It is true that the word choices and sentence structures of autistic writers often make it difficult to follow their thought processes. I believe that this is because most people are used to following one "logical" train of thought to what amounts to forgone conclusions. Autism spectrum people do not think this way. Rather, we constantly see divergent possibilities (and at a staggeringly fast pace) and our word selection and sentence structures often reflect this. Also, we tend to punctuate our thinking processes rather than the actual sentences we write. A comma, for example, is appropriate any time one pauses to think or stops to consider the possibilities of the sentence. Dashes often denote an important separate thought; perhaps seemingly unrelated, to the "normal" reader, but intimately connected in the autistic writer's mind. The thesis of the essay may seem to stray hopelessly, several times, only to come together in a poetic way with overwhelming strength at the end.

It is for these reasons that I have chosen not to edit the essays. On rare occasions I have changed the spelling or repaired a typographical error when it was clear that it was unintentional. Even in regard to my own contributed essay, I have, uncustomarily, let myself just write as I thought. I did not, for a change, censor or rethink what I put down. I allowed individual contributors to decide how long the introductions to their essays would be and what would be said about them. I also allowed individual contributors to decide the length and content of their essays. Though this may at times lend this work an uneven appearance, the contributors (and the editor) agree that the approach reflected in this amalgam is a truer reflection of autistic people and their lives. We are all different and all the same; a cultural composite.

People on the autistic spectrum do, indeed, have a culture—one separate from the "normal" world they must live in. Further, the autistic people who have contributed here have all expressed a belief that writing is the best way for an autistic person to communicate, and I agree. It allows time to form one's thoughts carefully, it has none of the overwhelming intensity of face-to-face conversation, and it affords the writer space to talk about one question or thesis without limit. For these reasons, I have treated the writings contained in this anthology as if they were ethnographic narratives. The result is their truth. Our truth.

In my introductions to individual essays, I have at times offered some commentary on what I believed were their germane points. My observations are just that, however, and readers are charged with finding their own "pertinences" in the essays. The patient reader will be rewarded not only with insight into the workings of the minds of autistic people (with an eye, I hope, toward improving their accommodation in the university community) but also with greater self-knowledge.

This is the first time that an autistic person has brought other autistic people together in an anthology to talk about our deepest feelings, insights, and hopes. Nowhere else will the faculty, administration, and service personnel of the university community find the kind of practical information and candid revelations held in this volume. There is simply no way for nonautistic people to gather this kind of information through questionnaires or interviews, or through reading what nonautistic people have said about us.

The people who contributed to this work were brave in coming forward. It is true that they knew they could write for me and I would understand them. They also knew, however, that you would be reading their words. I speak for all of us when I say that I hope you will be equally brave in turn, and use what we have given you here to improve the quality of life through inclusion for all people.

Acknowledgments

I thank my parents, to whom this book is dedicated, for their patience and support during my growing-up years; it is not easy raising a child with an Autism Spectrum Disorder. I also thank my stepson, to whom this book is dedicated, for without his life I never would have had answers for my own.

I thank my partner Tara, mom and dad Hughes, Davina, Holly, and Darcy. I would also like to thank Clare and my other autistic friends for providing me with a sense of community. Support and encouragement was always appreciated from my "normal friends" also: Mardi and Gene; Mark and Tina Lanci; Sue Lonac; Mark and Jennifer; Sherri Winans; Joyce, Susan, and the girls; John and Kathy; Stewart Brock; and Peter and Nan Fries. All of them have given advice and perspectives that made it into this book. I appreciate the sacrifices made by Hud Hudson and Beth Schille-Hudson; without them I would not have been able to write.

I extend thanks to Western Washington University, and especially my colleagues in the Department of Anthropology.

Introduction

Autism in the Academy

What would make a university student rock back and forth vigorously in an anthropology lecture, staring off into space, seemingly unaware of the discomfort of those around her? What would make a student bring a map of Hawaii to physics class every day, to place it carefully before him and study it intently? What would make a student get up from her library chair every five minutes and twirl in a clockwise direction three times, only to sit down calmly again? Why would a student ask a professor—in a very loud voice—the same question seven times in a row? Or take several weeks to complete a simple, two-page English assignment?

One might believe that students engaging in these behaviors are exhibiting signs of inattention, apathy, boredom, or worse: drug abuse, a rebellious nature, or perhaps a dangerous mental illness, leaving them completely out of touch and without any real connection to the society around them. The above descriptions, however, apply to university students with autism or disorders along its spectrum; students who, contrary to popular misconceptions, care deeply about connection; students for whom intellectual activity and a place in the academy are indispensable lifelines that give them the connections they need while providing an outlet for their unique intelligence.

As autistic students, our internal needs and motivations are often at odds with the physical environment of the university and many of its social and emotional demands. Behaviors that are "normal" to us (talking long and enthusiastically about our special areas of interest, disregarding personal appearance and sometimes hygiene, speaking plainly rather than censoring our thoughts) and our coping mechanisms (such as small rituals, a need for continuous clarification, an attachment to comfort objects) make us stand out as odd and sometimes unwelcome members of the university community. As promising students with special needs, we find ourselves being pushed from the one place that can maximize our potential and give our lives meaning.

Most people, whether they are a part of the university community or not, have beliefs about autism that are narrow at best. People tend to picture classic autism, or Kanner's Syndrome, the diagnostic criteria of which are as follows:[1]

A. (1) Qualitative impairment in social interaction, as manifested by at least two of the following:

(a) Marked impairment in the use of multiple nonverbal behaviors such as eye-to-eye gaze, facial expression, body postures, and gestures to regulate social interaction;

(b) Failure to develop peer relationships appropriate to developmental level;

(c) Markedly impaired expression of pleasure in other people's happiness.

(2) Qualitative impairments in communication as manifested by at least one of the following:

(a) Delay in, or total lack of, the development of spoken language (not accompanied by an attempt to compensate through alternative modes of communication such as gestures or mime);

(b) In individuals with adequate speech, marked impairment in the ability to initiate or sustain a conversation with others;

(c) Stereotyped and repetitive use of language or idiosyncratic language;

(d) Lack of varied spontaneous make-believe play or social imitative play appropriate to developmental level.

(3) Restricted repetitive and stereotyped patterns of behavior, interests, and activities, as manifested by at least one of the following:

   (a) Encompassing preoccupation with one or more stereotyped and restricted patterns of interest that is abnormal in either intensity or focus;

   (b) Apparently compulsive interest in specific nonfunctional routines or rituals;

   (c) Stereotyped and repetitive motor mannerisms (e.g., hand or finger flapping or twisting, or complex whole-body movements;

   (d) Persistent preoccupation with parts of objects.

B. Delays or abnormal functioning in at least one of the following areas, with onset prior to age three years:

   (1) social interaction,

   (2) language as used in social communication, or

   (3) symbolic or imaginative play.

C. Not better accounted for by Rett's Disorder or Childhood Disintegrative Disorder.

It has become clear since Kanner published on autism that the syndrome falls along a spectrum, classic autism being the most immediately identifiable, shading off into clinical pictures that are very difficult for people to notice in brief encounters.

As Francesca Happé has pointed out, it is people on the higher end of the autistic spectrum—people with high to superior intelligence—who are most likely to be able to come even close to passing for "normal," to being able to share experiences that many people take for granted, and to cope by utilizing their intellect and highly developed memory skills.[2] It is these relatively "invisible" autistic people who, by dint of their intellectual prowess, are most likely to find their way into the university system and then to be misunderstood as students who are detriments to the academy's goals: producing uniform students who learn well within a particular instructional range, freeing professors to engage in research which in turn brings the academy revenue and prestige. One thing that must be considered here is that the very professors who power a university may, at least occasionally, have an Autism Spectrum Disorder (ASD) themselves.

Though many are familiar with a type of professor often caricatured—absent minded, eccentric, lacking in social skills, unquestionably brilliant—high-functioning autistic students with these characteristics are invisible to the academy, even though the characteristics of high-functioning autism in children have been dubbed "The Little Professor Syndrome."[3] This invisibility in the academy is certainly not because these "little professors" turned older students don't exist; many a professor who fits this profile must have struggled through school to eventually find succor in the professional ranks of the academy. However, many brilliant students find the university a formidable mixture of overwhelming sights and sounds, full of change and disruption, and dependent upon social matrixes that are utterly mystifying. They quit university, never to return.

A vast resource of intellect and unique insight is thus lost. This is no small problem; though many people think of the term "autistic university student" as an oxymoron, there is evidence that a potentially significant number of students in the university system fall on the autism spectrum.

Many people are skeptical that autistic people could find their way into the university system. The skeptics continue to hold antiquated notions about autism and believe that all people with this diagnosis are bereft of communicative abilities, that they are completely unaware of their surroundings and have violent outbursts. Such outdated thinking fails to realize that there are many points along a continuum where autism is concerned. On the high end of the autism spectrum, an individual is often given a diagnosis of Asperger's Syndrome.[4]

Asperger's Syndrome was first recognized and documented by Hans Asperger, an Austrian psychiatrist working in the 1940s. Asperger's

young patients, all boys[5] exhibiting the same sets of sensory and behavioral characteristics, lacked the ability to connect socially and to
communicate effectively, engaged in perseverative behaviors, demon-
strated extremely narrow interests (to the exclusion of all others), and
had very high sensory sensitivities and prodigious long-term memories.[6] The DSM-IV outlines the diagnostic criteria for Asperger's Syndrome in this way:[7]

A. Qualitative impairment in social interaction, as manifested by at
   least two of the following:
   1. Marked impairments in the use of multiple nonverbal behav-
      iors such as eye-to-eye gaze, facial expression, body postures, and
      gestures to regulate social interaction;
   2. Failure to develop peer relationships appropriate to develop-
      mental level;
   3. A lack of spontaneous seeking to share enjoyment, interests, or
      achievements with other people (e.g., by a lack of showing,
      bringing, or pointing out objects of interest to other people);
   4. Lack of social or emotional reciprocity.

B. Restricted repetitive and stereotyped patterns of behavior, interests,
   and activities, as manifested by at least one of the following:
   1. Encompassing preoccupation with one or more restricted pat-
      terns of interest that is abnormal in either intensity or focus;
   2. Apparently inflexible adherence to specific, nonfunctional rou-
      tines or rituals;
   3. Stereotyped and repetitive motor mannerisms (e.g., hand or
      finger flapping or twisting, or complex whole-body movements);
   4. Persistent preoccupation with parts of objects.

C. The disturbance causes clinically significant impairments in social,
   occupational, or other areas of functioning;

D. There is no clinically significant general delay in language (e.g.,
   single words used by age 2 years, communicative phrases used
   by age 3 years);

E. There is no clinically significant delay in cognitive development or in the development of age-appropriate self-help skills, adaptive behavior (other than social interaction), and curiosity about the environment in childhood;

F. Criteria are not met for another specific Pervasive Developmental Disorder or Schizophrenia.

As we will come to see, at least some of the behaviors outlined in the diagnostic criteria of high-functioning autism and Asperger's Syndrome can become the underpinnings of academic success.

Which category a person falls into in terms of official diagnosis is based on the discretion of the diagnostician, minor (or profound) differences in speech acquisition, and other pieces of information given by the autistic person or family members and suggested by early childhood symptoms.

At the time that we as autistic people finally get a diagnosis—especially if that diagnosis occurs in adulthood—we are relieved just to know that there are others like us out there. Many people with autism care little for the fine distinctions of category, preferring to focus on the common underpinnings of the phenomenon.

At this point, one might ask how an autistic person goes undiagnosed until adulthood. Besides the fact that some of these syndrome classifications made it into the DSM-IV only recently, there are other factors. Most high-functioning autistic people, not knowing what is "wrong" with them, develop a lifetime pattern of using their intelligence to find ways to appear normal. The effectiveness of this strategy seems to improve with age. However, all of the autistic people I know (including myself) report that this strategy is not perfect and never hides our uniqueness completely. Like others who seek to be what they are not, we invariably end up with painful memories at best and self-loathing at worst. We push our memories aside as we grow older. Our parents may do the same. This is an unfortunate reality, because accurate memories of an autistic person's childhood and the histories of our symptoms are the very key to an accurate diagnosis.

Because Autism Spectrum Disorders can cause so much pain both to those individuals who have them and to their loved ones, much effort has been put into finding the causes of autism with an eye toward the eradication of the disorder. Many books and papers have delved into the genesis of autism and some have proffered "cures" for it.[8] Rather than focusing on the pathology of this condition, however, our purpose here is to share with the academic community real insights into the ways that we as persons with Autism Spectrum Disorders feel and perceive. Specifically, we discuss how these feelings and perceptions affect our struggle to contribute to the university system and how we contribute, through our considerable intellectual talent, to the enrichment of humanity. We make the case that by our very nature, highly functioning autistic people are irreplaceable members of the academy.

It is only recently that Autism Spectrum Disorders have begun to be more widely known not only to autistic people themselves and the professional community that diagnoses and treats these problems, but also to people who provide services to the disabled, such as the counselors, advisors, professors, administration, and disabled student services workers in the university. It is of great importance that these people begin to understand ASD through its commonalities as they endeavor to assist students in getting the resources they need.

Given the widely shared characteristics of people with autism, it would seem at first that anyone operating from the autistic spectrum would be an evolutionary dead end. The evidence provided by these essays suggests, to the contrary, that high-functioning people with autism actually have a great deal to contribute to our success as a species. Indeed, persons functioning on the higher end of the autistic spectrum may contribute revolutionary developments within their fields and propel humanity forward in key ways.

For example, many studies have linked eccentricity, unusual focusing capabilities, speech oddities in prosody and self-reference, and impulsiveness, unpretentiousness, arrogance, unsociability, insatiable curiosity, and a disregard for standard ways of behaving and thinking with intelligence, creativity, and divergent problem solving.[9] As we will see, these characteristics are present in people who are autistic.

The world has long delighted in celebrating strange but gifted people and incorporating them into popular culture; however, when confronted with these odd, brilliant people in life, society finds it difficult to cope with them. This is not to say that eccentricity, brilliance, and autism are one and the same. Rather, the essays in this collection illustrate that these features are often juxtaposed. The results of these juxtapositions present opportunities for individuals, their universities, and their communities to see things in completely new ways.

AQUAMARINE BLUE 5

GARRY

Garry was diagnosed with Asperger's Syndrome in 1998 by Dr. Tony Attwood at the Macgregor Medical Centre, Australia. A university graduate, Garry writes about the difficulties of his social life as an autistic person in the university. He tells us about problems that affect most people with an Autistic Spectrum Disorder: How do we go about making friends? How do we know when someone is being genuinely friendly? Why do our peers like the things they do? And most important: How much of myself am I willing or able to give up to fit in?

Garry's answer, like that of many ASD people, is that the stress and effort of trying to fit in are usually not worth it. The exhaustion and anxiety produced by trying to be something other than what we are leads to even lower self-esteem, falling grades, and depression.

Hello. I would like to introduce myself. My name is Garry Burge and I am 27 years old. I am here to inform you a little about Asperger's Syndrome and my life as a sufferer of this condition. I was diagnosed with Asperger's Syndrome in July of 1998 and I am presently coming to terms coping with this condition and trying to promote more awareness of AS (as I will now refer to it) within the community. I would like to describe to you what AS is, how it affects me, and how people like me with this condition can be valuable members of the community and good employees in a work situation.

I have often been asked by people how I felt in 1998 after I was diagnosed with AS. At the time I was very lonely, as I was attending my third year at the University of New England in Armidale and was living in a small flat on my own. I tried house sharing, boarding, and living in the UNE flats and none of these ever seemed to work. No matter how I tried I could not master the ability to make friends. I used to go for long walks and talk to myself as a means of self-talk and categorize my difficulties in making friends to the three strikes and you're out scenario—I will best describe them as: 1. I'd say "Hello"—2. Try to establish a conversation.—3. I'd be avoided next encounter. I used to phone home quite a lot and my parents, especially my mother, was aware that I was very anxious and quite depressed. My mother had been doing some voluntary work at a Primary School helping students with remedial reading and had under her care a boy who reminded her of how I was at his age. On mentioning this to the Special Ed. teacher she had just been given some material on AS. On reading it with my father, they had felt that the article was a description of me. On my arrival home on vacation, my mother suggested that I make an appointment with Dr. Tony Attwood to have an assessment.

After Dr. Tony Attwood diagnosed me with AS, my mother asked me how I felt. I told her I was so relieved to realize that I was not the only one with this condition and that a great burden had been lifted from my shoulders. On returning to UNE, I explained my condition to the counselor there and gave her a copy of my medical diagnosis. The counselor was not aware of AS at that time but had been seeing me once a week, after I had gone to her experiencing a panic attack one night earlier that year. I had needed someone to help me overcome my extreme loneliness and anxiety. She now followed up my diagnosis with the university staff and I was given assistance in being allowed to sit all my final year exams in a room on my own and the lecturers were more understanding when I approached them to make sure I was on the right track with my assignments. I had never missed a tutorial and they may have wondered why I never seemed to be a part of a group and always a loner.

I would like to describe AS, as it seems to me. It was as if I was like a seed frozen in time. The other seeds were growing and developing and I was getting further and further out of step and never looked like catching up. I had no insight into social conventions which regular people take for granted. This describes my 26 years as I existed in a world I did not understand. When my peers were making friends and enjoying companionship, I was protecting myself by sitting on the verandah at primary school, to escape the noise of the playground and the inability to be like other children. At High School, when not in class, I spent most of my time in the sanctuary of the library, where at least I could escape constant teasing, bullying, and worst of all rejection of the young teenagers to whom I was an outcast. At this time, because nothing was known about this syndrome, some teachers would in their frustration lower my already low self-esteem by saying, "I bet everyone will know the answer to this question but Garry." I retreated more and more into my own world and escaped my pain by de-personalization in the classroom, a removal of your mental being from the happenings around you, a type of survival technique.

My mother tells me, when I was young, that I did all the usual things at much the same time as my age group, such as walking and talking, but seemed interested in unusual things, sometimes way ahead of my years. When I was at preschool the teacher told my mother that although I could do most tasks, I did not show any interest in socializing with the other children. My parents decided that I should attend grade 1 and repeat that if necessary, if I was unable to cope. They always knew I was out of step and took me to various therapists and guidance officers but no one seemed to be able to pinpoint why I acted so differently. The consensus was that I was not retarded just somewhat different. I was very interested in the garden and I feel that that was probably my stress outlet. With AS it is very common to have obsessions.

While growing up some of mine were pocket watches, waistcoats, hibiscus, azaleas, roses, camellias, orchids, American presidents and politics. On my special areas of interest I would talk nonstop, unable to read the signals that my particular favorite topic should come to a close. Sadly, because of these traits and not being interested or able to do the same things as my peer group, I had no friends and now realize what I have missed out on, as I have no memories of having had friends and bonding with them. Because I had no idea of the social rules of behavior I felt extremely uncomfortable and became a socially unacceptable alien.

It seemed so much easier to talk with adults, as they were more tolerant. AS is best described as "a person trying to live in the regular world his or her own way." This seems distinct from autism, where a person "lives in a world of their own." Most, if not all people with AS are seen as odd or eccentric and peculiar. Because of their inept social skills they are seen as the "nerds" of society. People with AS want friends but they simply do not know how to interact or belong. I remember telling my parents that the rejection was much worse than the bullying and teasing. Life long rejection can make a person into a recluse and that is why early diagnosis is so important and vital.

I now help run an Adult Support Group. Some things which have come out of talking between members of the group that some of us share in common are extremely good hearing, frustration at not understanding how relationships work, sensitivity to touch, light, and sound, inability to tune in to more than one conversation at the one time, or to do multiple tasks from the one command, being mentally exhausted by trying to converse in a light or casual manner, not knowing how to react to social cues or body language, but most of all fear of rejection because we got it wrong. We have many varied interests and are relaxed in each other's company and some of the members of the group are actually gaining confidence and suggesting outings and contacting one another by e-mail or phone. I hope one day for friendships with regular people of around my own age and look forward to acceptance by them. I find myself studying young people to see how they walk, talk to one another, what interests them and how they dress.

I go back now to one of the best days of my life. That was the day I left high school in 1990. Now though arose the question of what I was going to do. Employment Services tried but could not find a job for me as I had had such limited success at school. In 1992 I enrolled in a Lorraine Martin College course. This course lasted 19 weeks and I learned how to touch type, use a computer, and gain some confidence. In 1993 I decided to repeat my Senior Certificate, only to be told that I would be unable to complete it, by an occupational therapist at CES, and worst of all not to even contemplate going on to university to undertake a Bachelor of Arts degree, which had become my goal. I can understand why they felt this way but I was determined that I would have a go and that nobody was going to make an assumption that I could not do anything. I wanted to do so passionately. I passed my subjects at Oxley College. Now I had my chance to go to university as a Mature Age Student and to undertake a Bachelor of Arts degree. This was the first step.

I was admitted to the University of New England in 1994 in Armidale. Now I thought at last I would be able to make friends with young people as they would be there in great numbers and I was going to live in one of the colleges. I had to leave home for the first time, arrange my timetable, choose my subjects, find out my mealtimes and find my way around a university and a new city. It did not take me long to realize though just how different I was. I now wondered if I could ever be like other young people. For instance I wondered if I could partake in the activities that other young men engaged in such as play football, or engage in rough and rugged activities. Or whether I could change myself by dressing like other young men who used to drive fast cars, wear curve-brimmed hats, roll their shirtsleeves up to their elbows, wear shorts or jeans and drink beer.

However, at the end of the day I knew this was not me. I really tried hard and wanted to desperately fit in with young people. At the end of 1994 I was to fail a full year load of university, which caused me to be excluded for one year.

It was after this that my self-esteem was at an all time low. I had tried so hard and now I did not know what to do. However, on arrival home and discussing options with my parents I realized that it had been such a big thing for me, with my limited background in education and, although this was a setback I would not give up. The university had suggested I undertake a tertiary preparation certificate. They thought failure was due not to lack of knowledge but how to write it down. Once completing this certificate I then reapplied to the University of New England and was readmitted there in 1996.

A new challenge: I had to find accommodation once again and after a number of failed attempts in UNE flats and house sharing and boarding, decided to live in a flat of my own. Some of the things I tried to do to relate to young people was to learn how to play squash and tennis. I had a go at indoor cricket, but found difficulty in catching the fast going cricket ball. I taught myself how to play tennis by drawing the layout of a tennis court on a piece of paper. I thought I would put what I learnt into practice and I joined a local tennis club in Armidale. Over time I managed to play tennis at an average level but once again I seemed to be out of it socially. The same problem occurred for me in squash and I ended up hitting the ball by myself against the wall at the squash court. I was still the outsider.

I joined a gym at university to see if I could build more confidence. The instructor's name was Steve. What impressed me about Steve was that he was a no-nonsense fellow who was self-disciplined with his gym exercises. He was a regular young man and used to play rugby and do all the usual things regular young men seem to do. I hoped he and I would become friends. However this did not happen. He was always very pleasant but I had to realize that because he was a public relations person, he needed to be pleasant to everyone. Even though I had tried to form a friendship, not knowing the social skills made it difficult for me to relate to him in a young person's language and caused me to feel frustrated when this friendship I had hoped for did not eventuate.

On 25 March last year, I attended my Graduation Ceremony with my parents. I felt so proud when I stepped up to receive my Arts De-

gree. Now my next step was to find employment. I went in and regis-
tered with the Commonwealth Rehabilitation Service. In March they
were able to get me a work-in-training position at the Parliamentary
Library for two months. After two months the library asked me to
stay on for a further two months to fill in for a staff member taking a
Long Service Leave. They knew of my condition and this was the hap-
piest time of my life. They were wonderful to me and even though I
still sat on my own in the canteen I still felt good about myself and felt
I was putting in a good effort which was substantiated when I got an
excellent reference from them. The positive side of AS is that we make
good employees. In the workplace people with AS like structure and
routine in employment, are punctual, can work alone, are meticulous,
pay great attention to detail, take pride in their work, do not talk during work time and do not take days off, and can handle repetitive tasks.
We tend to stay in positions for long periods of time and enjoy working
with people who are motivated and do not mind isolation. However,
it is difficult for us to interact socially with other employees and this
can give the impression that we are standoffish or aloof.

When my last day came, a morning tea was held for me and this
is a happy memory. Now I was unemployed again. I sent away e-mail
applications every day and went to many private agencies as well as
my Rehabilitation Services case manager. However, the private agencies advised me to say nothing of my AS. They did not know of it and
said, "You don't look like there is anything wrong with you." This created a quandary. When I sent my e-mail applications, I put only that I
helped run a support group for AS. If I didn't get an interview I always
left a brochure for their information. I understand that there are so
many highly skilled people looking for work, and these private agencies just don't have time to help someone like me.

However, in wrestling with this "to tell or not to tell," one of my
parents telephoned the supervisor at the Parliamentary Library to ask
her what she thought and she said, it had helped them to understand

why I would get very anxious if I made a mistake, asked many questions to make sure that I had it right, and understood why I did not find it easy to socialize and that it was not because I was standoffish or aloof.

I have tried to inform as many people as I can about AS and have written to many politicians. I have talked to counselors as they have some AS students, spoken to school principals, teachers, counselors, and parents, spoken to psychologists and generally have tried to inform as many people in the general community as I can.

At present I am going to an employment agency called "Pathways" who help people with disabilities and know of AS. They are helping me find employment and inform employers about Asperger's Syndrome. I believe there are employers out there who will give us a chance at employment as more is known and explained to them about our strengths in a work situation.

The AS group has grown in number from the original 4 to nearly 40 from the ages of 18–40 and we meet once a month for social outings. We are now starting to communicate by telephone and we are gaining confidence and at last know what it is like to understand the word friendship.

DARIUS

Darius is a man with Asperger's, diagnosed by a team specializing in autism in Leiden, the Netherlands, after self-identifying and then being referred to them by his therapist. Darius is a successful psychology student in a major European university. In his essay, he talks about the importance of context in learning for people on the autistic spectrum, a feature often missing in university instruction. He guides us through a variety of personal examples of his difficulties and successes within context, and argues strongly for the importance of diversity—another contextual component—both within the university and throughout the world as a whole.

My name is Darius; I am 38 and live alone in a large European city. I study psychology and work 20 hours a week (secretarial work). The rest of my time is divided between painting, community service, and social activities. I was only diagnosed with Asperger syndrome a few years ago. I diagnosed myself and then had the diagnosis confirmed by an autism team. This came about in a typically Aspergerish way. Basically, I got myself referred to them, told them about the latest research and the new sub-diagnosis of Asperger syndrome and that I thought I had it, and why this was so. They agreed that I had AS, but I couldn't figure out what they thought AS was. They probably saw it as another label for HFA (which it isn't in my opinion).

As was the case for so many high-functioning and/or Asperger syndrome people who were born in the sixties, an autism spectrum diagnosis was never even considered when I was a child. Our learning and social problems were ascribed to emotional problems or attributed to other illnesses or disorders. In my case, this was epilepsy, with which I had been diagnosed at two.

Childhood

Although I did not show the extreme behavior that is seen in classic autism, I did show many of the behaviors also seen in these cases, such as rocking and headbanging. I had extremely good memory and concentration for things that interested me but none at all for things I found pointless. I had special interests that hung around for a while and then disappeared to be replaced by the next special interest. I also acquired rather odd collections of things I wasn't even particularly interested in, but that happened to be collectible, such as TV Guide covers (though this is a current obsession). I still find it almost impossible to resist the urge to collect, if things come in series, though I am not at all into collecting the kind of things that are generally collected by neurotypical people, such as stamps. I used to collect stones and shards of pottery I found outside on building sites. I believed they were stone weapons and ceramics of Neolithic hut-dwellers. My mother, who at times had a distressingly down-to-earth approach to my hobbies, told me that they were just leftovers from people's picnics, but that didn't stop me.

Ever since I was young, I had extreme problems learning some things, while being extremely quick to acquire other skills. When I look back, I can see that quite a few of the problem areas had their basis in sensory processing difficulties and different cognitive strategies because of those.

My sensory channel that is most disturbed is probably the visuo-spatial channel. I have had problems with visuo-spatial processing as long as I can remember. This resulted in problems with practical and technical skills, as well as with orientation in space and visual recognition.

I found it difficult to learn how to tie my shoelaces and I somehow always ended up with my clothes on backwards or inside out. I got into the habit of simply getting inside my sweaters and then turning them around until they were on good side out and front-side in front.

Sometimes we were sent home early from kindergarten and since there was no one to pick me up I'd have to find my way home myself. I always got home, but it wasn't because I knew where I was or which road I was supposed to take. I just got out of the school building and started walking. I seemed to find my way by "feel" as if navigating by a sort of radar. It didn't occur to me to ask someone to help me find my way back. I never quite learned to find my way around the part of town where we lived. The neighborhood always seemed slightly alien to me and I was never quite sure if I had been there before.

In kindergarten I only learned to recognize some of the children and then only within the school environment. It was the same with the teenaged children of the neighbors who babysat for my parents. I'd know who they were in their babysitting capacity, but didn't recognize them when I met them somewhere else or I confused them with other people. When we moved to a different village and I had to go to a different school I treated some of the children who superficially looked like some of my old classmates as if they were those classmates. When my mother said that they were different children, I insisted that they were the same.

My visual processing deteriorates when I am tired or stressed. When I was small and especially in primary and high school I was stressed a lot. This resulted in some strange processing problems, one of them being a kind of "literalness in visual processing." I often seemed to process only the most basic visual information. I don't know how many times I have poured tea into the jar of marmalade for instance, instead of into my mug. I don't think "normal" people make these mistakes. Apparently I was capable of processing the visuo-spatial idea of "open" versus "shut" (the jar and my mug were both open containers) and perhaps size (they were about the same size) as well but not much more. Subtle differences, such as what was supposed to go into the respective receptacles, were apparently beyond my capacities at such times.

I also start to see things much smaller than they really are when I am tired. This is called micropsy. My vision remains clear, it even seems to gain in sharpness and clarity, but the objects and people become minute in size and recede into the distance. During my early schooldays I experienced micropsy almost permanently.

In kindergarten, I chose to play with blocks in order to try and remedy my defective visuo-spatial skills. I didn't really like playing with construction toys, but I thought exercising myself in this way might improve my practical skills.

During my early years in primary I took myself through puzzles of different levels of difficulty in order to get better at spatial insight. It didn't work. I was still hopeless at anything practical or constructional.

My hearing seems normal when examined by ordinary hearing tests. I hear everything and can distinguish between left and right when hearing with a headphone. My hearing is actually very sensitive. I hear the telephone when no one else does and I can hear the hum of electrical apparatus. This oversensitive hearing is often a problem because sounds that other people don't even notice are disturbing and even painful to me. I have huge problems filtering out what I want to hear. For comprehension, I tend to rely on context a lot. This type of hearing problem makes social life very tiring, because as soon as there are more than two people present, listening to conversations means having to put in a lot of effort piecing together what people might be saying. This means that I understand conversations best, when I already know the subject that is being discussed. Obviously, teachers are supposed to teach children what they do not yet know. Consequently, they put a lot of new information into their lectures. If you have this kind of hearing problem, learning becomes very difficult. You cannot use your coping strategies for finding out what is being said, because you cannot rely on already existing knowledge about the subject, to interpret lacunas in your actual hearing.

When I was little, I engaged in many self-stimulative behaviors. I used to rock back and forth, bump with my back against the back of the chair endlessly, and swayed my head back and forth at night in bed until I fell asleep. I engaged in self-stimulative behavior in public until I was about 11, when my schoolteacher stopped me one day while I was busy bouncing with my back to the wall of the bicycle-shed again and again during recess. He told me not to do it and I remember not understanding why I could not bounce, as it was such a reassuring feeling. I had already decided to stop publicly engaging in some of the more clearly autistic "stimming" behaviors and only did them in my room. This was the last one to go. I also had by that time learned to "disguise" some of the "stimming" and repetitive behavior. I sat for hours on the swing in our garden when I got home from school, for instance.

I was quite compulsively neat and orderly as a child. My room looked always the same, with my toys always lined up exactly the same way. I told my mother not to let the cleaning lady into my room, as she always put my things in a different order on the shelves after she had cleaned them. I even offered to clean my room myself. I knew this was not normal and I envied my friends who had rooms that looked lived-in and who felt free to play and make a mess in their rooms. Years later, when I cleaned house to support myself during my study, I worried about not knowing exactly where to put the toys of the little boys, but then I realized that other children aren't as obsessive about the place of their toys as I had been. When I was fifteen I taught myself to leave clothes and books around the way normal kids do, because I recognized that it was not normal to have a room that was so completely neat and orderly. To actually start re-structuring your behavior consciously because you recognize its pathology is in itself rather abnormal behavior for a child. I have always found that kind of reflexivity quite normal, but all the doctors I saw during childhood used to be astounded by my apparently abnormal level of introspection.

Primary

My deviant cognitive processing led to all sorts of learning problems
and social problems, as well as to some assets from the academic point
of view.

Like many children with a diagnosis in the autism spectrum I had
an extremely mosaic pattern of skills and deficits. I would come up
with detailed knowledge at unexpected moments such as the dressing
habits of the Chinese under the Manchu Dynasty. At night, in my bed
I philosophized about such things as to whether being an ergative
languages-speaker leads to different perception of the self, the problems of giving an exact definition of a chair, and what the artistic requirements of a poem in sign-language might be.[1] In stark contrast
with these rather precocious skills and interests, I was unable to learn
some of the more traditional things on the curriculum such as arithmetic and topography.

This kind of scatter in skills and deficits always seems to make
teachers suspicious. When you enthusiastically display your knowledge
about some arcane subject, they think you are showing off or trying to
humiliate them. When you do not have certain skills considered appropriate for your age, they suspect you of being lazy or trying to sabo-
tage them, because apparently you are capable of learning other rather
difficult subjects quite easily.

Because visual stimuli are not processed properly by me, I have
learned to rely heavily on context. My brain works very associatively
and so I use context to set the associative process going. Once I know
what the context was, I can generally get back much of the original
knowledge. This means that many of my learned skills (especially those
based on visual recognition) are extremely context-dependent.

In primary, we had to learn topography and we had to learn this
at home. The next week we had to take a test. I failed abysmally. The
map at home had different colors. When I learned from the map at
home, it was lying flat on the table. The map in school hung down from

the ceiling and the background (table versus wall) was also quite different. Because the placement of the villages and towns on the map was not processed separately from the color and the background, I could not recognize those towns and villages on a different map and in a different environment.

I also had piano lessons and for years, I had problems playing on another piano than our own or the one in the music school. I knew of course that other pianos were essentially the same, but somehow I could not find the central C on a piano that had a different color, and I had problems finding the right keys on a piano that played heavier or lighter than our own piano. The size of the keys also differed marginally on different pianos and this confused me as well.

Today, it is assumed that visualizing problems for autistic children will help them learn, but this may not be the case for all forms of autism. Visual stimuli simply don't enter my brain in a meaningful way. This was probably the reason why I used to talk to myself all the time. I translated everything explicitly into language. I still do this, whenever I am stressed.

I also seemed to learn the other way around. Most neurotypical children are taught simple procedures first and when they manage those, they go on to ones that are more difficult. Only much later is the rationale behind those procedures explained, if at all. You are expected to learn the "tricks of the trade," not to actually understand the reasoning behind them. Because I had great difficulties with arithmetic and later with mathematics, I was given remedial teaching.

This didn't help at all, because this is based on the idea that children have difficulties understanding the more difficult problems. It is assumed that in order to teach, one goes from problems that are simple to problems that are more difficult and there is consensus about which type of problem is simple and which type of problem is difficult. Therefore, when a child experiences problems learning it is naturally assumed that it doesn't understand the more advanced aspects. There is nothing wrong with the level of my understanding, however. It just needs to get a different type of input and be given the opportunity to use different learning strategies. This is because due to my different cognitive processing I do not experience the same problems as "simple" and "difficult" that other pupils do. My math teachers never understood why I could not do the sums that were needed to solve a problem, whereas I was perfectly capable of explaining how you had to solve a particular problem. When they had exhausted their teaching tricks, they generally ended by telling me that I didn't have to understand the formulas. I just had to learn them by heart and then use them during exams, as everyone else did.

For me, this didn't work at all. Any kind of learning that is based on "cramming" instead of understanding never seemed to stick. I think this is rather typical for people of the particular autistic brand I belong to. I needed to learn higher math before I was able to retain simple arithmetic rules and learning the tables was a disaster. I could recite the Greek alphabet and entire children's books when I was three, but I had huge problems learning the tables when I was nine.

Some of the cognitive problems I could solve through other means, such as a powerful focus of attention and a great memory. For instance, I solved my topography-learning problem by learning it entirely anew during the ten minutes we got before the test, during which we were allowed to rehearse what we had learned. I zoomed in on the map during that short time. Then I took the test and got an A. I have a great memory. Of course, that type of learning is no good in the end, because it isn't stored in long-term memory. To this day, I am often clueless about the whereabouts of particular cities.

I also learned to keep talking and ventilate as much unusual detail and general knowledge as I could think of, so as to appear really well-informed. If you prevented teachers from asking questions, they might never notice the lacunas in your knowledge. The smokescreen of knowledge will prevent them from noticing that you haven't answered the questions they did ask. Luckily, neurotypicals are not too good at noticing inconsistencies in other people's communications (or their own, for that matter).

Teachers also thought I was easily distracted. They were right, but it was not the type of attention problem most children have, which is that they can't focus and have a short attention span. People with that kind of problem are easily distracted by external stimuli. People like me are—as Asperger himself noticed—distracted from within. We have a very interesting inner thoughtscape and can daydream for ages. My associative thought processes led me to ideas and possibilities much more interesting than the subjects taught in school. Daydreaming occurred most during subjects I was not very good at. I'd have to wait ages before getting help with a sum. The teacher would show me how to do the sum and I'd have the same problems trying to make the next sum. Waiting between sums gave me many opportunities for daydreaming, especially because I became less and less inclined to ask for help.

I created elaborate fantasy worlds and I had a whole separate life in those imaginary worlds. Apart from self-invented fantasy characters and fantasy characters from books, real people such as Mozart, Christopher Columbus, Leonardo da Vinci, and many others I happened to hero-worship, also populated these worlds.

One teacher put me in a separate room to do my sums, because he recognized that I was easily distracted. Unfortunately, because my problem is generated from within this only made things worse. Having no external distractions whatever made daydreaming even easier.

High School

When I was in high school, my learning problems seemed over at first, because I did very well in first grade. From the second grade on things deteriorated again.

My educational difficulties followed the same pattern as in primary.

At first, I could hide my problems by simply using intellectual coping strategies, but when things got too advanced, I couldn't hide the lacunas in my knowledge any more.

Some of my visuo-spatial problems also became more noticeable in high school.

In primary, we always sat in the same classroom, but in high school we had to change classrooms for every subject. I have to know a particular place forwards, backwards, and sideways before I start recognizing it. Lighting and time of day/year also make a difference. I never knew to which classroom I had to go next and simply followed the other pupils around. I was not only disoriented in space because of problems with recognition, but I also didn't use external, visual evidence to orient myself. I spent a whole year in high school before realizing that room NR. 303 means the room is on the third floor (300) and in the left wing (odd nrs).

The only advantage from having to change classrooms was that it facilitated the attention change to another subject. Like many autistic people, I have a "sticky attention-focus."

Most classrooms also had fluorescent lighting and my brain simply goes into jelly-mode in such an environment. If you are experiencing learning problems due to innate cognitive differences, you do not need an environment that makes learning even more difficult. Fluorescents also give me a headache and headaches are not conducive to learning either.

The problem with context-dependent learning became even worse, probably because of the fact that we now did most of our learning at home (in primary we hardly had any homework). I had great difficulty accessing knowledge I had learned at home during tests at school and had terrible grades most of the time. The only good grades were in subjects that required understanding rather than rote learning. As long as I could reason my way through tests, I had no problems. I could use my associative thought processes to retrieve facts, but the associations I make are not necessarily the ones that teachers make or writers of studybooks have in mind, so this would not necessarily work at that point, as I had not yet learned to make a structured use of my associative processes. My tendency to think associatively rather than linearly resulted more often in a loose, rambling sort of style that could not be controlled and used in a constructive way. Consequently, it was often impossible to locate and retrieve the needed piece of information.

Social Problems

My social problems seemed over as well at first. In the first grade I was confident and liked by my peers; I was even chosen as spokesman for my class, because my fellow students appreciated my analytical powers and debating skills in dealing with teachers.

The different children in my class were from all kinds of backgrounds and of various levels of ability. Diversity works well for me, because my own differences from the norm are less visible in such a situation. After the first grade, we were channeled into different academic flows according to our abilities. My social problems were much more noticeable among children of the same social class and ability.

I soon acquired the reputation of being an eccentric and original, due to my odd social behavior and my rebel attitudes and dissident remarks in the classroom. Half of the students hated me because in general people hate individuals that force them to question their own personality or lack thereof. Older students sometimes approached me to tell me that they admired how I apparently wasn't afraid to stand out in the crowd. I was the only student who confronted other students when they circulated totally unfounded rumors about a gay teacher[2] and told them to shut up about the private affairs of others. To this day, I hate the kind of showing off with other people's private life, which for neurotypicals seems to be a normal ingredient of everyday conversation. I never could understand why anyone would want to parade their lack of interesting thoughts, the fact that they have nothing to say for themselves and lead completely uninteresting lives, and therefore need other people's private lives to have at least some conversational topics. I also stated rather bluntly in a class full of orthodox Christians that any god that limits heaven to people who go through the right moves (baptism, going to church two times on Sunday) instead of to those showing the right behavior (any decent person of whatever religion) cannot be a very ethically advanced or caring one. I wasn't out to be a rebel or a dissident. I just didn't see why a person should not say what he thought about a certain topic. I always was completely frank about what I thought and never understood why people would be angry because of that. After all, I didn't get angry with people who disagreed with me either! I only argued with them until I was satisfied that they understood what my point was. They didn't have to agree with me. Other people however often misconstrued this argumentativeness as wanting to be right.

I remember making faux pas after faux pas. Of course quite a few of these social dos and don'ts were in fact not social at all and had very little to do with sensible rules or true empathy. I had no lack of empathy nor did I lack insight in ethics or morality. Arbitrary rules and social fashions, however, simply eluded me. One day I told my fellow classmates that I had visited my grandmother in hospital and explained that she had cancer. Everyone looked at me as if I had been caught masturbating in church. After a short but eloquent disapproving silence, they rebuked me: "You don't tell that kind of thing. . . ." Something like "don't mention the C-word" is the type of "social rule" that has to be spelled out to me. Of course, I would probably not adhere to that kind of rule even after having it explained to me. Treating a disease as if it were a cardinal sin that cannot be mentioned *"en plein public"* is too ridiculous for words. Social mores resulting from moronic prejudices like that will not find me an avid pupil. I'd probably end up putting my foot in it anyway, if only to try to break silly prejudices like that.

When I was a teenager, I suddenly experienced a period of echolalia in which I would repeat other people's social comments and mimicked their behavior. I only did this in situations where there was a distinct social interaction going on, never in situations where the conversations were purely informational. It was an entirely involuntary reaction, as if I was forced to try and be part of a social interaction by imitation.

Some people have commented on the good imitations autistic children are capable of. In my opinion, this is also a context-dependent learning-effect. I used to relate what my grandmother had said in exactly her words and tone of voice. My family thought I had a great sense of humor, but I wasn't trying to be funny. Content and form were inseparable to me and this was the reason I repeated the message verbatim and in her voice. It is a bit like singing a hit record by a particular artist in exactly the same style and type of voice.

My social life was also made difficult by the fact that I did not recognize faces. It would take me the entire year to get to know the people I was in the same class with. When I finally knew who was who and was able to recognize them, not only when they were in their seats, but also in the corridors, the year would be over. This had been less of a problem in primary, because it was a small school and I stayed there for six years. In high school, there were 10 first grades and once I got into the fourth grade we weren't in classes anymore but had our own individual schedule. We'd have different classmates depending on which subjects we were attending.

I used to have problems following children's programs on the TV, because it made it hard to follow the story line. I kept forgetting what had happened to whom. I mixed the characters up all the time and also didn't recognize them in different outfits. Other people only had to cope with a few main characters; for me they were multiplied by at least three times, because of this recognition problem.

Not recognizing your surroundings and the people around you, is like living in a social and environmental fog. It uses up a lot of your energy just navigating around, finding out what your position is and in which direction you are supposed to go next and whom you have to approach or avoid.

Literal speech is often mentioned in connection with autism. It is supposed that this literal speech is somehow special and the symptom of an autism-specific problem. People do not seem to notice that literal speech occurs in other disabilities as well, such as in schizophrenia and blindness. Nor do all autistic people have a problem with it or if they do, it may not be due to the same underlying problem. It seems to me that being literal because of sensory stress problems is a different (and perhaps more treatable) problem than being literal because one is primarily a visual thinker and has problems thinking in language. I myself am hardly ever literal and then only in social situations that are chaotic from a sensory point of view. Nowadays, whenever I make a literal reply I generally realize I have taken things too literally, even while I am replying.

I do have problems assessing what exactly is meant by a purely social type of remark. Other people seem to have no difficulties with that. For instance, when someone says: "Let's go to the swimming pool," other people always seem to know whether this is an invitation to them personally, or merely intended for some of the people present. I never know whether I am invited or not. People would have to explicitly invite me to come too. I often do not notice when people are only saying things in jest, unless they use a literary device, such as a certain way of phrasing. If someone asks me, "Why didn't you do this or that, you know you should have," but only means to tease me, I often reply as if the question was literally meant. I do not have problems with literary types of ambiguity, only with the social type. Sarcastic remarks are not lost on me, because there are often linguistic differences compared to "normal" communications, whereas ordinary social teasing can only be decoded within and through the social context. The sort of nasty remarks gay men make, for instance, depend on using a different tone of voice, or on using very elaborate or ultra-refined phrasing, so I always get those. Gay men are also much more direct of course. They say what other people only imply. Example:

> Woman: Is that a new dress? I really love the colors and the pattern is very nice. . . .

(Subtext: of course you are too fat to be wearing that kind of design, let alone such colors.)

Gay man: Did you knit that sweater yourself? Very intricate design . . . very clever of you darling . . . but blue isn't really your most flattering color, is it?

I am very good at these kinds of communications myself. That's not surprising because cutting remarks derive their effectiveness from clarity and precision, qualities much valued by autism spectrum people.

My communication skills also depend on how many people are present. If there is not too much sensory chaos, I am much better at decoding social behavior than when I find myself in a noisy group of people in a small space. When there are more than two people present my appreciation of all the possible cues to interpretation quickly deteriorates.

Living Independently

When I was in high school the idea of having to work and earn a living really frightened me, because I was well aware that I would have problems functioning in a work environment. However, since my academic record wasn't too great either there were few other options. Because I was officially diagnosed with epilepsy, I had little chance of finding a job anyway. Unemployment rates were skyrocketing and if you had a disability or a chronic disorder, you were legally bound to mention this to your future employer. With jobs being scarce people like me had very few chances of finding one. Because I had no idea what kind of job or career I wanted anyway, I spent the first few years working in volunteer projects in other countries. I loved living and working abroad. The volunteer jobs were not too interesting from the work point of view but at least you were working together with other idealistic people. I also loved learning different languages and my social problems were less obvious in such an alien environment. The natives would assume you didn't know the ins and outs of their specific culture anyway, so they would not be surprised if I messed up socially. For the first time in my life, I actually had a social life, and for the first time I did things together with other people (other than the sports activities I had been sent to by my parents). These years have built up my social confidence considerably.

My sensory problems and consequently the learning and social problems still exist.

I still engage in self-stimulative behavior, but I make sure no one notices. I still rock, but only within the confines of my own apartment. I always make sure the curtains are closed so the neighbors can't see me. I do have to monitor myself, for excitement generates an auto-matic "stimming" response and when I am in a public environment I have to check my impulses. Things like opening and closing one's hands or stretching your fingers or even handflapping are not noticed by most people, but I prefer to be on the safe side.

I still have the same context-effect problems and they occur in a variety of recognition-tasks. A street entered from the south is a differ-ent (and to me unfamiliar) street than the same street entered from the north. A person wearing black trousers and a gray sweater is not recognizably the same person when wearing jeans and a red pullover. When I started learning to use a computer I had huge difficulties using a different computer (one that worked in the exact same way) than the particular one I had learned something on. The simple fact that it faces another wall is wildly disorienting to me. This leads to an "alien experience" and from that to non-recognition of the task/procedures to be used.

Social Life, Sex, Relationships

My friends tell me that when they first met me, the social oddities were very noticeable, but after a while they had the impression that my social behavior improved. I told them that this was very unlikely. I probably had become used to their personal ways. I can learn to be al-most normal with a certain person or in a certain environment. If the environment changes I have to learn everything from the start again and the same is true if I meet someone new. Social learning does not transfer to different people or situations.

Nowadays, I don't literally imitate the other person's social behavior anymore. Rather, it has developed into a kind of "free improvisation" on someone's personal interaction style. This means that I look gauche with socially inhibited people, but can look deceptively normal when in the company of someone with good social skills. My best friend noticed this when I stayed at his place. Within the space of a few hours, two friends of his came by. I was silent and rather shy with the first and easygoing and talkative with the second. Apparently, the change in behavior was very conspicuous.

I still have problems in groups where there is too much information going on, or where the informational flow is too fast. I simply can't shift my attention focus quickly enough to the relevant part of the interaction process. Consequently, I miss a lot of vital information needed to interpret social messages. There is no such thing as adequate delayed social reactions. One either is quick enough to keep up, or one is weird and socially disabled.

One consequence of my sensory processing difficulties has to do with experiencing emotions. Because my visual channel is so disturbed, it needs an enormous amount of energy to have it function at even a basic level. This means that I have no energy for most other things, such as emotions. Having to process the visual reality generally leads to a suppression of any emotions that might be present. This has some odd consequences.

I am a great person to have around in the case of accidents and the like. I remain cool as a cucumber and am able to deal with everything quite effectively, because due to the visual stress, my emotions are suppressed and cannot get in the way.

On the other hand, flirting is a problem. As soon as I have to stare into someone's face, I am no longer able to feel the doting feelings that generally are supposed to go with this behavior. This makes the first stages of love very difficult, as I am no longer able to feel anything for the other person, as soon as I interact with them visually. Because to other people, experiencing those feelings is the main drive to go on with the relationship, I don't often proceed past the first stage. Why go on with doing something that is mainly stressful? This visual stress is most strongly present when I don't know someone that well, or in situations where I am very close to the person.

I had similar problems when my best friend was dying of multiple sclerosis. I found it hard to listen, look, and talk at the same time. I also experienced severe micropsy, a sure sign of stress. I solved this, by explaining this phenomenon to him and I also started to write him letters. During the two years before he died I wrote to him weekly. I have no problem expressing my emotions on paper at all. He liked this way of interaction because he was often tired as well and he could read my letters whenever he felt he was up to processing them (MS also takes its toll on the brain).

Another consequence of this way of processing is that I can manipulate how much I want to feel, when I am watching television. When I don't want to experience the emotions that are generated by for instance certain items on the news, or horror movies, I only have to turn off the sound. Where I live, most programs are subtitled, so I would still be able to get the information. Because it now goes through the visual channel the emotional impact will be entirely gone. Only hearing and smell generate emotions in me. The only emotions I am able to feel through vision are those that are the result of beautiful nature and beautiful art. In a social environment visual experiences don't generate any emotions in me at all. Sound and smell, on the other hand have an enormous emotional impact on me and I am quickly emotionally overloaded through those channels.

Because the visual world is not very accessible to me, I still tend to overlook visual clues. Some time ago, I went to the library to return a volume of a psychology journal. I was reading the labels on the various series of journals to find where mine had to go back. Then this girl passed me and she looked rather puzzled. I looked to the volume in my hands and the ones in the rack to see if something was wrong. Only then did I notice that the rack had only series of psychology journals bound in black in them. The volume in my hand was sky-blue and obviously shouldn't go in that rack at all. Since I am so verbal and non-visual it had never occurred to me to look at the type of book, instead I only read the names on the back of the journals.

My recognition and consequently, my learning, are still extremely context-dependent, unless it is learning of an extremely analytical and abstract, conceptual type.

My face-blindness and context-dependent learning make for some hilarious mistakes. When I enrolled in a painting class (drawing the male nude), I had the experience that made me first question my face-recognition skills.[3] When I went there for the first time, I didn't know all the other students present. We sketched for about three-quarters of an hour (three poses of 15 minutes). Then we had a break and I walked around the studio to see how my efforts compared to those of other students and to become acquainted with at least some of them. A boy I hadn't noticed before started to talk to me about painting and what kind of paintings I did normally. We talked during the entire break. Then the teacher announced the break was over and we took up our positions behind our easels again. My conversation partner undressed and went back to the center of the studio, where he had been posing previously. I had not realized I had been talking to the model, because I had not recognized him with his clothes on! This was so obviously the kind of mistake no person with normal recognition skills would be likely to make, that I decided my brain must be processing the environment in a radically different way.

During my first year in university, I regularly came across a girl somewhere in the psychology faculty building. I didn't have a clue who she was, but apparently she knew me, so she stopped to chat. After that, we often talked when we met in the corridors or in the elevator. I learned to recognize her in the faculty building. I knew of course several other students. One of them was a boy who majored in astronomy and minored in psychology and he and his girlfriend used to join my friends and me in the bar.

It was only somewhere during the second year that it suddenly dawned on me that his girlfriend and the girl I always chatted with in the elevator were the same girl! This experience is even much stranger than you might think at first glance, because it isn't just about not recognizing her in these two different situations. For to me, she was two different people and so I had a different relationship to "both," for I regularly had conversations with the "elevator-girl" but never said more than "hi" to the "bar-girl." She must have thought me a very strange guy, or perhaps she just thought I was shy in company, who knows?

I do see similarities between persons very easily. I recognize the category but not the individual. There exists, for instance, a certain type of intellectual/trendy gay man, very recognizably gay to other gay men, though not recognizable as such to most straight people. My therapist was a variant on that particular prototype. He once said, very perceptively, "When I come to fetch you from the waiting room, you seem to know who I am, but you give the impression of not really recognizing me individually." That was a very good observation. Of course I knew who he was, as I had come to the clinic to see him and naturally assumed I would see him and not some other psychologist or even a different specialist. I would not have recognized him if I'd met him in a different environment, say, in a gay bar. I might have said to myself: "That fellow over there looks a lot like Jan" and I might have considered the possibility that it was he, but I wouldn't have been sure. After all, entire gay choirs look like that. I have at least three other friends who are slightly different variants on the same prototype. This is the reason why I am not a very spontaneous person. I always wait to see if the other person recognizes me and then try to find out unobtrusively through "sowing" several discussion topics who the person is. I might introduce ballet and if the person reacts, I know that is where I know them from, if not, next topic until it clicks. As soon as I know the context, I can usually make out whom I am talking to. German accent + Talmud class = German fellow student sitting opposite me. German accent + talks about "Johnny the Irishman," "granny" or "those Indian gay guys next-door to you" = German girl living in apartment underneath mine. I also see an image of the original context and I can scan this to see if the person I am talking to is present.

Another consequence of this face-blindness is that it can take some time before I start to experience some continuity in my experiences with people and relationships. "Normal" people build up their relationships with people based on the experiences they have with them. The nature of the relationship changes for better or for worse with every new experience. In my case, this only starts to happen after a longer period. While the other person is building up a behavioral image of me in his mind, my experiences of him are scattered over several "different" people and are therefore not integrated into one experience of one particular person. For this reason, relationships tend to stay rather one-dimensional until finally a person becomes one of my more intimate contacts. If a person stays on the fringe of my social life, I may never develop a "rounded" view of his personality. NTs would have developed some appreciation of that person's individual characteristics by then.

Of course over time, I learn to recognize people by the topics they talk about or by the surroundings where I am more likely to encounter them. If people have very recognizable characteristics such as being extremely tall, extremely fat, or being the only Maori in town or whatever, I learn to recognize them fairly quickly.

I am currently living on my own. I have had relationships but never felt I could live with someone permanently.

Sexual relationships have several "problem areas" for autistic people. First, we need a lot of solitary living. Anyone with severe sensory perception problems needs time off from the stress of social interaction. I have heard people with hearing or sight impairments say the same. I couldn't live with another person permanently unless the house was big enough and we had our own living areas.

Physical intimacy can be a problem, as for most of us touch is also affected. I don't like soft touches. They give me the willies. Temple Grandin said that autistic people, like animals, are reassured by firm touch and I can only agree with that. I used to have problems sleeping in the same bed with someone else. I am able to do so now, but the bed has to be big enough, otherwise I feel too stressed.

I also don't like kissing. The first time I did it I thought: Why in heaven do people like this? This is very strange. Is it long enough already? What does one do next? Insert tongue into other guy's mouth; right! I remember it took some time before I figured out that the reason I almost choked to death was that I forgot to breathe through my nose. Strange, because I do breathe through my nose, like everyone else, so why not during kissing?

I have had both girl- and boyfriends but consider myself to be predominantly gay and I think being gay is a decided advantage from the communication point of view. Women are much more given to saying what they do not mean and meaning what they do not say. Female communication patterns drive me up the wall. Gay men are much easier to talk to as they are much more direct.

My autistic relational style is actually less of a problem among gay men than that it might have been if I had wanted a straight relationship. Many of my gay friends also feel that they do not necessarily want to live 24 hours a day with their partner. The kind of relationship arrangements that are often seen in the gay scene, such as living in one house with separate quarters, or having a sexual relationship with one person and a close emotional bond with another, suit me perfectly.

Obviously, before one even gets to the actual sex or relationship stage, there is the flirting. This is a major problem for most of us. I have had to learn this consciously. I am now able to decode the flirting process when I see it happening in other people but I still cannot do it myself. When I see a man looking at me, I never quite know what I should deduce from that. At first I always interpreted this as a look of disapproval; perhaps because my clothes weren't trendy enough, or some such judgment on my looks or behavior. It took me a while to figure out that the rather aggressive, hard stare gay men use on other gay men is a sign of interest and not a sign of disapproval. I also found out that men and women have different flirting styles. Men stare and women laugh. At first, I thought all those women were making fun of me for some reason or other. Having Asperger's does make one terribly paranoid. Small wonder, because most of us have suffered bullying to some extent and are therefore not inclined to take other people's good intentions for granted. Although I now know what that kind of stare means, this doesn't mean that I know with any certainty that it is intended for me. With my visual problems directions are never obvious and whenever I intercept such a stare my first reaction is to look around to see who the pretty boy who must be at the receiving end, is.

I have heard that some people with autism used sit-coms in order to learn about social behavior. They liked the fact that they were so predictable and repetitive. I never really did that, perhaps because I have AS and consequently am more high-functioning in the language department. To anyone with good verbal-analytical skills, ordinary sit-coms (especially most of the American ones. Sorry guys!) are an insult to the intellect. Anything that insults my intelligence is not likely to amuse me. It is the very repetitiousness and predictability of those incredibly one-dimensional social jokes that never progress beyond the most basic levels of subtlety and which are the main ingredient of those programs, that puts me off. The only ones I find amusing are the more absurd English ones such as *The Young Ones, Are You Being Served, To the Manor Born, AbFab,* and *Fawlty Towers.*

The only American sit-coms I like are *Married with Children* and *Family Ties.* The last one I really only liked because of Michael J. Fox. He was absolutely brilliant in portraying the somewhat disconcerting Alex Keaton-character, who had some definite AS characteristics, if you ask me. The way he wove together the rather absurd world of Alex

Keaton with the quite ordinary behavior and expectancies of the other characters, was very convincing. Instead of acting "look how funny I am" he acted "look how normal I am." He managed to make you almost but never quite forget that Alex was really a rather odd person and that his ideas and solutions to problems were ever so slightly out of focus, all the time. It was this "normality manqué" of Alex Keaton which made the series into more than just an ordinary sit-com.

Social life is, apart from being stressful and irritating, also rather absurd to most people with AS. It is the logical consequence of having good ethical and moral insight, good analytical and verbal skills, and little natural feeling for ordinary social skills and social communication. It can't be a coincidence that so many of us enjoy Monty Python and other forms of absurdist amusement.

I like the English sit-coms better on the whole, because they tend to stress the absurd much more. Especially Basil Fawlty's social life is very recognizable to me. I once said to my English teacher that I felt I had much in common with Basil Fawlty. He immediately denied this. After all, Basil Fawlty was simply crazy and I was not, he said. I had mixed feelings about this. On the one hand, it shows that my coping strategies work quite well and I am not noticeably weird anymore to most people. On the other hand, it also makes clear how invisible the enormous efforts we put into acting normal are to other people. I hope this essay will help make them appreciate these efforts more. Watching sitcoms like *Fawlty Towers* and *To the Manor Born* is painful as well as hilarious. They are sometimes a bit too close to the truth about social life as I experience it. Especially the frantic efforts of Basil Fawlty to make things work, as well as his obviously stressed life because of trying to remain one step ahead of disaster, are a bit too much like my own. Perhaps some people feel that this cannot be true as *Fawlty Towers* is so obviously absurd and does not happen in real life. I think however, that it is an excellent, if magnified, portrayal of life as an Aspie. It has to be a magnified portrayal, or "normals" wouldn't even notice that something odd was going on.

Social life for a person with AS is rather like having a homunculus in your head, which is a cross between Basil Fawlty and the civil servant of the Ministry of Silly Walks. While you are on a date or having a conversation with your boss, this Basil Fawlty–homunculus is frantically silly-walking around in your head, interrupting your best efforts to act normal with deafening and incessant shouts of: "Don't mention the war . . . Now, don't mention the war!" I have a love-hate relationship with my homunculus, because I suspect that normal people also have a homunculus in their heads, but that these are simply extremely boring and not much fun to have shouting in your ear, all the time. So I'll just have to put up with mine and make him keep his voice down a bit.

Work

I work part-time, because I need a sizeable proportion of the week to "reload." It is not the work itself that is a problem, but having to be around other people is very tiring for me.

The first weeks in a new job or indeed any new environment are generally hell to me. It still takes me at least a year but generally longer before fellow-students or coworkers start to look familiar. It took me over a year before I could differentiate between the three secretaries of the manager of our department. They were all blond, thirty-ish and about 1.70 meters tall.[4]

I explained my recognition-problem to my coworkers, but people simply don't understand until I actually walk by them on the street without recognizing them. My colleague told me that she heard how people thought I was arrogant because I didn't greet them in the street. She had to explain to them all over again that I didn't recognize them and therefore probably didn't realize they were someone I was supposed to know.[5]

The first few weeks in a new job I have to put so much energy into processing all the new information that it takes an enormous effort to process enough information to know how to do the task one is expected to do. I am generally quicker than others catching up with all sorts of knowledge and skills that require analytical understanding but I need a much longer time to get used to different telephones or copiers or to know where to find what. During the first few weeks, I simply don't process my environment beyond the most superficial visual level. Someone who tries to explain something to me in a new environment should take his time, because I can't filter out the relevant from the nonrelevant sensory stimuli when there is too much new visual stuff going on.

This not only shows in having to retrain myself for much longer on the practical aspects of a new job than anyone else; it is also evident in my hearing and seeing. When I am doing something and another person starts talking to me it simply doesn't register. I may hear every word he says but it doesn't sink in. Consequently, I might not react to anything that is being said.

During my first week of work in a high school, I had to sort the mail and bring it round to the lecturers' room. When I entered the room there was only one teacher in the room and I started to distribute the mail. I heard him talking while I was checking the names.

"You are new here, aren't you? Where exactly do you work? Are you one of those foreign work-students . . . Hey, I am talking to you . . ."

By then another teacher had entered.

Second teacher: "I don't think he is hearing you."

Actually, I did hear everything, but the meaning simply didn't sink in. It never occurred to me that those perceived words were a communication directed at a person. Even less so, the fact that the communication was directed at me, even though there was no other possibility.

I also do not hear depth. By this, I mean that when there are different telephones in a room and they are all in different places, I cannot hear which of them is ringing (unless they have different ringing sounds). To me they all sound the same, because I cannot hear whether

34

the sound is coming from the right or from the left, whether it is be-hind me or in front of me.

These processing problems make work so tiring for me. After a while I learn to "wall off" the distracting stimuli to a certain degree and pay attention only to what needs to be attended. This only works for as long as the relevant and nonrelevant stimuli stay the same. When they change, chaos reigns again. This explains why many autistic people prefer things to stay the same. If you were blind, I'm sure you would also develop a "preference for sameness" for the placement of the fur-niture, for instance. I don't want the furniture of the sensory stimuli moved around too much either, because it makes it difficult to navi-gate the social and learning environment in much the same way.

University

Three years ago I decided, that what I really enjoyed was thinking about the human mind, language, and philosophy. I missed using my intelli-gence, so I wanted to get a university degree. In the end I opted for psychology, as that would give me a thorough research education as well as sound basic knowledge in all the subjects I was interested in. Since A-levels in math were a requirement for a university study in psy-chology, I decided I would simply have to pass the math exam. I used to get terrible grades in math and I now think this has something to do with my lack of visuo-spatial orientation. To me, numbers have a dis-tinct spatial side to them and this makes it difficult for me to process and remember them properly. I studied by identifying precisely what types of mistakes I made. Then I stated these explicitly every time I did sums. I found that I am not lacking in the abstract, analytical-thought department, it is the number part that is my undoing. My method of study worked. I passed my exam with the highest grade of all 34 stu-dents (only 4 passed).

This shows that I have learned to use coping strategies effectively or I wouldn't be where I am now, because I am by no means "cured."

The perception processing problems and the cognitive differences are still present and these have effects on my learning that I have to deal with. Some of these problems take different forms now, or are less obvious to the unsuspecting onlooker.

My hearing problems are less of a problem now, because I attend the much quieter evening lectures, instead of the noisy day lectures. Occasionally I have to take day lectures and I am always very tired afterwards. After three hours, I am absolutely wiped out from straining to understand what the lecturer is saying.

Because the world we live in has changed considerably compared to the sixties and seventies and has become a lot more visual and technical, some new problems have come up while others have become less acute precisely because of those technical advances.

The light sensitivity is a problem in an environment where there are a lot of computer screens and fluorescent lighting about. I need a special screen so I can't use the computers at the computer lab, or if I have to, I end up having a royal headache.

On the other hand, my problem with slow writing is now a problem only when I have to take exams. Papers must be done on a computer or a lecturer won't even look at them. I am a slow writer but I can type extremely fast. The problem with structuring papers is also made much easier by the use of computers. I am a great fan of the "cut," "copy" and "paste" modes on the computer. I still remember the old days with lots of drafting and rewriting by hand and I am thankful that those days are past.

I also have learned to make a more active use of my associative thought processes when I am studying. Instead of waiting for them to spring into action during exams and have all kind of undesired effects, I manipulate them and try to make as many idiosyncratic associations as possible, for these work best. I study in several different environments to minimize the context-effect.[6]

Another rather unexpected advantage of autism is better communication. I know that we are supposed to lack in communicative competence, but I don't agree with that. This is too simplistic a view of communication. There are many different types of communication and they do not all need the same skills. It is important to distinguish between purely autistic communication problems and communication problems due to other disorders (such as retardation or hearing and vision impairments). Not all people with autism are impaired with respect to all aspects of communication. Social communications are difficult for us, because they often have as priority not to explain something, but "bonding" between conversational partners or taking the emotional temperature of an interaction. You have to be able to use all your senses simultaneously in order to "see" the web of action that together makes up a certain pattern of social behavior that has a specific meaning. If you cannot do that you either miss vital information or you take things literally. This is also the reason many of us have difficulty lying. Social skills are at the basis of good lying skills. You need to be able to weave these webs yourself. This is an illusionist's skill. A good illusionist has to be faster and more dexterous than his public, for this is the only way in which he can get them to believe in his reality. It stands to reason that as most autistic people are slower interpreting and weaving social webs, they will not be good liars.

In actually getting a message across NTs aren't very effective communicators. A lot of their communication is faulty because either nothing is being communicated, or something unintended is communicated. This is not just the case in communications that are meant to be purely informative, it also happens in so-called emotional communications, where the real message is not what is being said explicitly (the informational level of the message), but what is implied (the underlying emotional or social level). The person on the receiving end more often than not is lacking in listening skills. This means that this person probably wouldn't understand even a perfectly communicated message. From the purely communication point of view this is a disaster scenario. So-called normal communication is just as defective as autistic communication. The mistakes made in "normal" communication are simply so omnipresent that nobody notices them anymore. That doesn't make NTs communication patterns more effective than autistic ones, just different.[7]

I have often noticed how teachers do not listen to what students really are asking and consequently do not give an informative answer. After the lecture, I have to explain to my fellow students what the "real" answer to their question is. Most people don't really answer appropriately to what has been said to them. They simply go off like alarmbells in a completely predictable way, repeating old reaction patterns to perceived slights or attacks.

I have noticed that the answers I don't get during exams are never the really difficult ones. Rather, they tend to be the easy ones, where I saw a solution or a problem that led me to give a different (but not necessarily wrong) answer instead of the "correct" one. I also give "wrong" answers to questions that are badly phrased. Apparently neurotypicals, perhaps because they all make the same communicative mistakes, do not notice the messed-up, noncommunicative quality of these questions. They may be able to take them to mean what the teacher meant them to mean (which, to anyone with good analytical thought processes and language skills would not be obvious at all) because they not only think in the same way, but also think the same kind of things.

If your focus is different, other people have to be clear about what they mean. If they are not clear it is impossible for someone like me to simply assume that he probably means the kind of thing I would also mean, because it simply wouldn't be true most of the time.[8] Whenever I try to find out what in heaven the question is supposed to be, I often end up with the wrong interpretation and because of that, with the wrong answer.

Because of my different attention focus and because of my associative thought processes I often have an unusual and original point of view. An attention focus that highlights other aspects than the usual ones can be of great value to any researcher. Associative thought processes lead one beyond the confines of one's own intellectual territory and this makes it possible to find new and different solutions using other

fields of knowledge, or to ask new questions that are not obvious to
experts in your own field of expertise. As Hans Asperger himself said, it
depends on other qualities of the autistic person, such as overall intelligence, whether these cognitive differences lead to original but non-
constructive dead ends that are merely deviant or whether they result
in perceptive questions and innovative solutions.

Though autistic thinking is generally equated with rigidity and in-
flexibility I wonder whether this nonlinearity in some aspects of thinking isn't also a positive quality of the autistic mind.

Certain aspects of autistic thinking can therefore actually be an
advantage as they may lead to new insights and creations. One of the
comments made most often by my teachers is that I have shown a criti-
cal attitude toward the subject and advanced some interesting new ideas
and approaches. Skills needed in the academic world such as logic, analytical thought processes and not being smoke-screened by smooth-
talk (very useful when reading articles about research) come easy to
high-functioning autistics. To be able to dissect arguments and to be
able to untangle problems and explain them in an easy and understand-
able way is also a quality that is much admired by other people.

When I am writing papers for my courses, I have to take into ac-
count that other people do not think in the same way that I do. It takes
a bit of extra work, as I cannot simply assume, the way most people
do, that the other person is like myself in most respects and will have
the same type of emotional and cognitive responses to a certain event
or piece of information I'd have. Having had to acquire this skill instead of being able to simply assume that I can use my own thoughts
and thought processes as a model for those of other people is a huge
advantage. It means that you are less likely to fall into the trap of
believing that you know what other people are experiencing, simply
because you (think you) know what your own experiences are. This is a
great help when reading research articles and interacting with patients.

These "theory of mind" skills[9] we are supposed to be lacking in,
are not really so widespread among NTs as experts on autism like to
think. The theory of mind skills of most NTs are entirely dependent

on the fact that they are so completely average and most of the people they will meet during their life will most probably also be completely average. There is no true merit in knowing what another person feels if the other person and yourself are entirely interchangeable. People like that run into problems as soon as they are required to imagine what someone with another background might be experiencing. Watch a few talk shows if you don't believe me.

Not being average is also an advantage when one studies the human psyche. I have had many of the so-called abnormal thought processes mentioned in the literature myself. This means I am able to think about the possible problems and assets associated with them much better than healthcare people. Most of them have never experienced what their patients experience. I know what it feels like to be severely depressed or hypomanic. Like many AS-people, I have first-hand experienced many of the thought disorders associated with OCD and schizophrenia. This doesn't mean I have actually been psychotic. It is important to distinguish between having strange cognitive experiences such as those seen in schizophrenia and bipolar disorder and autism and failing to distinguish between the common reality and the one that is created by these deviant cognitive experiences. If experiencing the symptoms would be enough to be called psychotic, many people with epilepsy and migraine attacks would also have to be called "psychotic." In my opinion, it is the construction of a whole new reality around those symptoms that is the psychosis.

I think that having autism prevents one from being sucked into the psychotic reality even if one experiences these symptoms. When I was a child I was able to observe my own mind while these odd thoughts (that seemed to exist outside my own person but within my own mind) happened. It is this detached attitude towards one's own mind and soul Hans Asperger described so well, which may protect autistic people who do experience some of the symptoms seen in blatant mania and schizophrenia. I was never frightened, only intrigued at what the mind can do. It is the same for other symptoms such as feeling "open" (having the experience of an expanding sense of self, of consciousness, that includes the experiences of trees or the wind or having one's sense of self fall away into the bigger consciousness of the universe). For a future psychologist these are invaluable experiences. When talking to people who are schizophrenic or who are manic depressive they always forget that I am neither. Apparently, the way I can talk about these symptoms convinces them that I know what I am talking about.

Overall, I don't regret what I am. I may experience problems because of my different sensory perception and cognitive system, but I see and experience many things that other people have to experience by proxy, through art, or have to have explained to them by introspective and verbally gifted people. I think life would be very boring if I were normal. I don't envy neurotypical people. I asked people with schizophrenia and bipolar disorder, and many of them felt the same. As a psychologist, my focus will not be on "curing" anything (not just autism). Instead, I'd like to understand (I am terribly curious, and simply want to know why people think and react as they do). I also want to help people live with what they are and turn their problems around to work in their advantage, rather than change them into Jane or Johnny Average.

There is much more to tell and explain about how high-functioning people manage to deal with everyday life, but that would take an entire book. For the moment, this will have to do.

This essay not only explains how my mind works, it also shows how my thought processes work, through the way it is written. I have structured it somewhat (as to make it easier to understand), but not as much as I would for a paper, because I thought it might be more interesting for readers if it showed the original line of thinking.

Polishing the text further would no doubt have made it smoother, the change in subjects less jerky (from an NT point of view). It would also have ironed out many of my autistic thought processes, such as the associative thought processes. On the whole, I think that leaving traces of this autistic thinking process is more interesting than trying to sound completely neurotypical.

I also feel a perverse pleasure in making you work for your information. There is some justice in the fact that you will have to adapt to my idiosyncrasies for a change, instead of me having to spend a lot of energy trying to figure out what you are about. Are you feeling tired and somewhat confused and do you have the disconcerting feeling that you have missed something, but do not know what and where? If you do, that may actually be the most valuable effect of this essay on you. It will make you appreciate the energy we have to put into tuning in to you.

I hope it also gives some insights to those who have been wondering what life on the high-functioning end of the spectrum is like. I also wanted to make it clear that I wholeheartedly agree with Dr. Hans Asperger, who felt that autism should not be eradicated, but that people with this syndrome can make a valuable contribution to society. Believe me, you don't want to erase the autism gene from the human gene pool. You'd end up with something much worse than having to cope with the occasional autistic person. You'd end up with only neurotypicals. These might be entirely "normal," but they would also lack most of the skills and talents that make life such a great experience, as I firmly believe these skills are closely tied to things like autism, schizophrenia and the like. Always remember: AUTISM ROCKS *SOCIETY!* And society needs rocking badly.

> *Respectfully yours,*
> *Sincerely yours,*
> *Greetings,*
> *Be well,*
> *God bless you,*
> *Blessed be,*
> *Keep the faith,*

> *Darius*

(I never know which sentence to use. Since the social skills of most of you, my readers, are probably better than mine, I'll leave it to yourself to choose the ending phrase you feel most comfortable with.)

MICHELLE

Michelle is a woman from the University of Texas with Autistic Spectrum Disorder. She was diagnosed three separate times; the final report—given in college—offers a definitive diagnosis of Asperger's Syndrome. In her essay, she talks specifically about her odd eating habits, a feature sometimes shared by ASD people. Her writings remind us that not only are autistic features likely to show up in unexpected places—in this case the school cafeteria— but that, again, misdiagnosis of ASD can stretch as far as Anorexia Nervosa. The psychiatric field recognizes that there is a possible link between autism and Anorexia Nervosa (see S. Fisman et al.'s "Case Study: Anorexia Nervosa and Autistic Disorder in an Adolescent Girl" in the Journal of the American Academy of Child and Adolescent Psychiatry *35 (1996): 937–40); however, the field fails to recognize that one of the most salient features of clinical Anorexia Nervosa—an unrealistic picture of oneself as obese—is absent in ASD.*

As university counselors have become appropriately more aware of the needs of people with eating disorders and continue to field referrals in this category, they should be advised to look closely at a person's motivation for odd eating habits and not rule out ASD. Michelle's essay sheds important light on our eating motivations, histories, and experiences.

Her essay also shows that some people on the spectrum can and do have social relationships.

I've always been incredibly picky about my food. Well, "picky" is how my mother always put it—other people have used other terms. Friends, coworkers, shrinks have called my eating behavior everything from eccentric or compulsive to anorexic or bulimic to just plain weird.

At home, it wasn't that big of a deal. By the time I was 5 or so, my mother would let me eat pretty much what I wanted—as long as I fixed it myself and I didn't eat too much junk. When I was younger she tried the whole "battle of wills" thing a few times, but she discovered pretty early that I could be stubborn all day when I needed to.

When I was around 3 or 4, she told me that I couldn't leave the breakfast table until I finished my orange juice. That night, I was still there and so was the orange juice. Soon after, I caught on to the fact that she wasn't willing or able to restrain me all day, so I'd just get up and leave when I was done, regardless of what was said. Again, my parents learned something about me—not to make any threats or deals that couldn't be carried through to the extreme.

Looking back, the orange juice incident is pretty typical of my food "issues." The color, texture, and variety of the foods I eat have always been more important issues than taste. In terms of texture, I like all my food as smooth as possible—the orange juice had pulp. I also like as little variety in a meal as possible. When it comes to color, I don't eat red foods, and if there's more than one food of the same color in a meal, they should taste the same. I always had cheddar cheese for breakfast, and the taste of orange juice after that would make me anxiously angry—it just felt wrong for anything exactly the same color as cheddar cheese to taste so different.

Given my preference, I'll eat just one food at a time—having several small snacks rather than big meals with multiple foods. I also don't like to have more than one type of food in my mouth at a time, although I can handle up to 2 or 3 sometimes if I have to. Casseroles, mixed salads, and stir-fry are definitely foods I avoid. Sometimes you're in a situation where you just have to eat that mixed salad—then I just pick out the pieces of lettuce and eat them separately, then the croutons, and then I leave everything else.

There were the occasional exceptions of course. Pizza never

seemed to bother me—it didn't matter that the sauce was red, or that crust + sauce + cheese + sausage added up to more than three. And sometimes I'd make these great sandwiches, with peanut butter spread on the bread, and Cheese-It's arranged in a perfect 3 × 3 square, with raisins at every intersection. If someone had just jumbled all those together, there's no way I would have eaten them—but arranged like that, they were pretty good.

As a kid, little quirks like these only got me labeled as "picky" at home, but eating at a friend's house, or at the school cafeteria, was a different matter. The looks and stares I generally wouldn't notice unless someone pointed them out, but all the questions really bothered me. People, misunderstanding the nature of my "pickiness," would try to force me to try different foods. Even today, having someone say, "Here, try this!" while waving a forkful of something in my face results in a huge wave of anxiety.

The older I got, the more I adapted. By middle school, I had a routine down where I would simply order the exact same thing every day in the school cafeteria (a slice of cheese pizza, a dish of yellow corn, and a carton of white milk). This looked normal enough to the other kids, if a little boring, that they'd ignore it. Even so, I'd find every excuse I could not to eat in the big cafeteria. Although my meal was nice and routine, it sometimes upset me to see so many hundreds of kids eating so many different things all at once. The rest of my meals were at home, where I could relax and eat the way I wanted to.

My comfortable routine hit a big crack while I was in college. I was in a dorm, which meant that all three meals a day had to be in the big, bustling cafeteria. To top it all off, there were almost no foods that were consistently available, every day, at every meal. For the first few months, I found all sorts of ways around the problem. I became a vegetarian, because the vegetarian meals were generally simpler fare than the standard meals. I tried to eat at off-hours, when the cafeteria would be less busy and nerve-wracking.

Unfortunately, the more friends I made, the more people there were to start commenting on my eating habits. There was no escaping it—we weren't allowed to take food out of the cafeteria, and there was always someone I knew around, and inevitably someone would start saying something about my eating.

The more stressed I became about eating, the more rigid my eating habits became. For a few months, I reached the point where I would only eat one food all day, or even for several days at a time: nothing but bagels, nothing but Cheerios, nothing but pasta, nothing but popcorn. If whatever it was wasn't available, I simply wouldn't eat. Hunger was never really an issue—even today, I'm the kind of person who sometimes forgets to eat on weekends.

Anyway, my friends, watching all this, decided that I must be anorexic, like the girls in the made-for-TV movies. After a couple of weeks of telling me continuously that I wasn't fat (which struck me as odd, as I had never thought I was), pressuring me to eat more, and monitoring every bite I took, they finally "turned me in" to the school counselor.

I received a short and sweet lecture on how all my friends really cared about me, and how they wanted to help me. Then she got down to business—it was a matter of shape up, or ship out. I was told I had a couple weeks to start eating "normally," and warned that she had people watching me all over campus. If I didn't "improve" by the deadline, I'd be sent to the locked psychiatric ward of the hospital across town. Of course, we all knew kids who'd been sent there—and none of them had ever been allowed to come back to the school.

Well, the pressure was certainly on, but all it really did was send my anxiety through the roof. I took to rolling up into a little ball and rocking under the tables again, something I hadn't done much since preschool. Finally, I decided that if I could force myself to act "normal" socially (which I'd been doing for years at this point), I should be able to make myself eat normally as well. I hauled down to the cafeteria, got a tray with a vegetarian meal, sat down with a group of people, and ate everything on the tray.

Ten minutes later, I was in the bathroom, vomiting it all up. I hadn't planned for it to work out that way, but the mass of anxiety and frustration that welled up inside me, knowing that I had all those different foods in my stomach, all at once, was just way too much. My dad used to always try to get me to eat everything by saying, "It all ends up in the same place!" This time it sure did—it all ended up flushed down the toilet.

For a little while, this worked. I was seen eating normally often enough that my friends and the counselor unanimously backed off. At this point I started to relax a bit, and was probably a tad less cautious than I should have been. Out of the blue one day, a guy I knew—not really even a close friend—came up to me and told me had made arrangements for the two of us to eat breakfast together the next morning, before the cafeteria normally opened. Afraid of being turned in again, I went.

He had piled some food on a table, the kind of foods I'd normally eat, and just sat down and started eating and talking. Talking, but not about me, or how I ate funny, or how I was mentally ill, or anything like that. Just talking. We finished as the cafeteria was opening, and I left and got ready for my first class. And that was it.

Now, I don't mean to say that I suddenly started eating three full meals a day just like everyone else. But I had suddenly discovered—Eureka!—that the "everyone must eat every meal in the cafeteria during designated eating hours" rule was not an absolute. It was now something that I could potentially adapt myself around. And I did. Oh, I still ate cheerios every morning in the cafeteria for breakfast, but there was nothing about that to be considered too weird—after all, lots of teenagers don't eat breakfast at all.

Plus, I started stocking the dorm fridge with some staples from the grocery store across the street—frozen burritos and ramen noodles. Every night for dinner, I could have one of those. There was a microwave, right there in the dorm. Admittedly, most people just used it for late-night popcorn, but it worked just as well for burritos and ramen. And lunch, I compromised, and ate pseudo-normally in the cafeteria. I made sure I always ate some kind of vegetable or fruit plus something with protein in it. The meal still just had two items in it, but they were the kind of items that said, "We comprise a normal meal," to everyone who looked.

It all sounds pretty simple now, but seeing the alternative options was definitely not one of my strengths. Back then, it seemed like my only two options were to either drive myself crazy trying to eat like everyone else or simply stop eating altogether. It took someone else stepping in for me to stop and look beyond the black and the white.

Frankly, the 5 years I lived in dorms were probably when I ate the healthiest. Now that I live on my own, I don't make such compromises as often. I make some attempts at normalcy—I keep a wide enough variety of foods stocked in my kitchen so that it looks normal to friends or visitors. But, most of those cans of soup or frozen dinners will never be eaten—there are probably less than 20 foods I eat at home on a regular basis. And even now, I tend to revert to my "one food only" routine when I'm especially stressed or anxious—nothing but bagels, nothing but toaster pastries, nothing but pizza or popcorn.

Occasionally I'll make a concession to nutrition and eat a jar of baby food vegetables. I actually tried pulverizing my own veggies in a blender for a while, but it wasn't worth it—they don't taste any different than the baby food, they don't last as long, and I don't like to touch raw vegetables or see them sitting in the fridge with my normal foods.

And actually, I have learned ways to eat completely and utterly normally every now and then. After all, if you're having dinner at your boyfriend's parents' house, or lunch at a job interview, it is definitely not the time to amuse them with your eating habits. I've been told the technical term is "dissociation"—I just completely distance myself from the fact that I'm eating. It won't work for a huge meal, and I have to keep the distance up for quite a while after I've eaten, and it can be pretty exhausting, but it's gotten me through some situations.

I even ate a sandwich once that had two kinds of meat, plus lettuce, tomato, and mayonnaise. Of course, I've since learned that it can be socially acceptable to remove the tomato. You can't remove the meat, or scrape off the mayonnaise, but you can take off the tomato. Some things I will never understand.

Oh, and the people watching me eat don't bother me so much anymore. If they make some comments about my eating, I just smile and ignore them. If they wave food in my face, I claim to be allergic. And if they still keep pestering me with questions about my eating habits, I just smile and remind myself that autistic spectrum people aren't the only ones with some social skills deficits.

CROCUS

Crocus is a college student who, after seeing many professionals, went to a diagnostician who believed that autism could explain many of her challenges. Crocus reminds us that "spiritual autism" is far worse than physical autism. Her writing also serves to help those in the university system, whether that university is a secular or a religious institution, that students are complex weavings of both body and spirit. Undoubtedly campus religious counselors will have contact with autistic students with unique needs spiritually, psychologically, and practically.

This essay is unique in that it challenges the notion that autistic people have no refined feeling for things outside themselves, no complex understanding or feeling of connection to God. Crocus shares with us her ability to identify deeply with Christ and understand Christian teachings in some ways even more profoundly than "normal" people.

I am a 25 year old college student who was born with "half the symptoms of autism." I navigated through the special education system under such labels as "learning disabled," "communicatively handicapped," and "emotionally disturbed." I was mainstreamed fully into the sixth grade but my struggles to understand the mystery of myself were continuous until I was diagnosed with several newly discovered brain conditions by a progressive neuropsychiatrist (a seizure disorder of "brief 3–30 second blank spells" that are undetectable on an EEG and attention deficit disorder—inattentive subtype). This diagnosis happened two years after my graduation (with honors) from a good private Christian university with a bachelor's degree in art psychotherapy.

In doing his evaluation, the psychiatrist could not rule out Asperger's Syndrome. As I have begun to be more aware and understand things that for years have been a mystery to me, the common thread that has held me together is my faith. Indeed, it has been the most important key to coping with the mysteries and misunderstandings that I have dealt with as an autistic person. Hence the title . . .

On Spiritual and Physical Autism

Last night, I had a dream. In the dream was a teenager from my church, now become a man. He was autistic, and he was trying to get me to explain to him the social rules for dealing with a specific situation. We were in a building vaguely reminiscent to me of our old parish hall at our church. Before I could respond I woke up with a semblance of an answer on my lips.

It might seem strange for me to begin my essay on what it has meant for me to be a university student, who is Christian, with an autistic spectrum disorder, with a dream. But the intersection of dream and reality, internal worlds and external worlds that have had everything to do with my life as a student, a person with a pervasive developmental disorder, and last but not least as a Christian. For those of you reading this who are not Christian, I want to reassure you that my primary purpose of this piece is not to convince you of my beliefs, but rather to offer a general challenge to those within the Christian community, of what it means to have an autistic fellow believer and student in their midst. I want to remind you that it is far worse to have "spiritual autism." It is to flesh out what I mean by spiritual versus physical autism that I have written this cautionary tale.

The Wonder and the Horror

It is my premise that at the heart of being a Christian is having both a wonder and a horror about what it means to be human. And that at the heart of many misunderstandings between autistics and the "church" is the all too human error within the ranks of religion to emphasize one extreme of human nature over another. When we retreat to extremes, and get away from the relational mandate of Christ, we begin to acquire a form of spiritual autism. Autism literally means "self-involvement." When it comes to the physical condition of autism, my personal observation is that the literal meaning of autism is less than adequate—but when it comes to spiritual autism, I am reminded of my own soul, and what it means to have this condition separate me, and separate others, from truly being in relationship with a personal God. A God whom I have experienced in a physical, palpable, if you will, incarnational way. A God who, unlike many with spiritual autism, is unafraid of entering into the labyrinth of my mind. A God who can live with the wonder and horror of being human, having taken on flesh and blood Himself—and experienced both life and death as a result.

This incarnational, relational faith that is deeply embedded in who I am has always been at odds with institutions that seek to control and order this God of mine. Institutions that have sought for religious and other reasons to control and order the mystery in me. Institutions that have sought to play God—a lonely, stereotypically "autistic" deity with more concern for modifying behavior or following a seemingly arbitrary rule than in seeking a Power outside of themselves to change their heart and mine.

Until shortly after my college graduation, I was unaware of the full nature of the mystery within me. And it was my Christian faith that enabled me to endure the consequences of not knowing. Despite what I have said about the ordering and controlling of mystery, there is a certain clarity when you know when the mystery begins and ends. It means that you are able to come to terms with the mystery of your life and with a different mind.

The Mystery

> *Lunatic fringe on the edge of the shore*
> *A wave of untouchables floods the back door*

Trying to gain a mystery explained
Yearning not to be ignored.

It seems I was born reaching out for divine mysteries. The human ones seemed unsolvable and too painful to gaze at for long. One of the chief human mysteries that I lived with was knowing ever since I was able to speak for myself that I had been born with "half the symptoms of autism," and that I had a "pervasive developmental disorder —not otherwise specified." I guess I figured I could deal with a God who did not pretend to be fully explainable more than I could a condition that the doctors were not willing to admit was a mystery. The closest they ever came to admitting this was stating that my case was "highly complex." And who wants to live their life as "not otherwise specified?" I was sure that I didn't.

My Attic

Lunatic fringe in that attic of water
Gasping cold bubbles, shivering thin
Stretching stark hands in a stiffened ocean
Of coddling counsel and tidal wave friends.

I began to reject the medical profession and most of humanity entirely. And I worked hard to overcome this mysterious entity: half the symptoms of autism. Whatever that meant, I knew I didn't want it. After numerous visits to neurologists, specialists, and speech therapists, I began to have independent speech when I was six years old. But independent speech doesn't mean that you know how to introduce yourself or that you know your own phone number or even that you know the difference between the "f" and "th" sounds. Or that you know the unspoken rules for talking on the phone and inviting classmates over. God didn't seem to care about what I knew or didn't know about communicating. He had been misunderstood, even rejected, by His own people when He was human. And when I stretched out my hands toward Him, He was more than willing to embrace me. I later learned that the word for that experience was "grace."

Division, Fear, and Combat Shutdown

> Lunatic fringe on the edge of the shore
> A wave of untouchables floods the back door
> "Where is the depth of division that burns
> Between us and the ones who can soar?"

Underneath my rejection of the human race was an utter confusion and terror as to how to deal with them. It was physically painful for me to make eye contact—why did people look at each other so casually? It seemed like such a callous invasion. The same was true of human touch—it all seemed so maudlin and overdone. By the time I began to be OK with eye contact and human touch, I was asking questions and not knowing when to stop. The emotional torture from my peers when I did this, ensured that it would be years before I began to speak up in a group of people again.

In my third-grade Sunday school class, there was a boy who was deaf. He was learning to talk and pronounce words around the same time that I was. We both encountered the same teasing, and the same impotence of the teachers, who despite their kindness did not know how to stop the verbal abuse that went on. I began to realize the depth of division between us and the "normals." It was around this time that I began to shut down emotionally entirely—at least at school and church. By the time I was in sixth grade I was well on the way to regarding God's "eye-contact" as too painful to bear.

> Close your eyes and you won't have to cry
> Careful now to turn away from Jesus' surveyors
> Bend oh bend those ever weeping-eyes
> Mummify Methodically the soul's portrayers
> Sleeping over weeping any time
> Close your eyes and cry through snores of intermittent sorrow

Perhaps I'll find a land that's beyond time
A land that will be walked upon tomorrow.
Close your eyes and you won't have to cry
Careful now to turn away from Jesus' surveyors
Opening those ever-weeping eyes
Would mummify my memory's portrayers.

In my relationship with God, I found a land beyond time. I vividly imagined Jesus sitting beside me, as I rode on the bus to a school outside my neighborhood, with a different special education program. As I encountered the taunts, the profanities, and the fist-fights of children and teens with every conceivable mental disorder and emotional disturbance, I pictured Jesus was with me. In doing so I found a way of escaping the realities in front of me. It was the realities in front of me that would intrude, and lead to my later frustration and anger with God.

And yet, even in the anger, even when I would kick God away, I found His love for me to be constant. Unafraid to enter the labyrinth of my mind.

In direct contrast to this was the spiritual autism I encountered from many in the institutions that shaped my life. Textbook definitions state that autism is characterized by repetitiveness, rigidity, and an obsessive desire for "sameness." Books have been written on children with autism who construct their own world out of a desire for self-protection, and on the attempts of high-functioning adults such as Temple Grandin and Donna Williams to build a bridge between "my world" and "their world." The reality of spiritual autism is often lost in the process. I have observed this obsessive desire for sameness and preserving the status quo in many of the specialists who saw me in the schools I attended, and the hospitals I visited for evaluations. There were psychiatrists and psychologists who would write in their reports that I had no capacity for being creative, when not one year later I would begin writing poetry and drawing and show my capacity for being creative in the most irrefutable form. They made the naturalistic assumption that because they could not see their version of what "creative was," it therefore did not exist in me. They construct a religion out of the Stanford-Binet IQ test, and despite the fact that my score showed a wide scatter of abilities, they accepted the final score which was considered "borderline mentally retarded" as the final statement on my "mental functioning."

Years later I would read these evaluations and weep, but even at the time of these evaluations, in some unexplainable way, the negative, "spiritually autistic" attitudes of these people were evident to me. They had made their IQ test a false God and bowed down in deference.

Another reported characteristic of autism is a lack of empathy. Professionals were afraid to enter and explore my world, except perhaps to psychoanalyze, pathologize, and "fix" my internal universe. Except for one brief stint overnight for a sleep-deprived EEG to determine the presence of seizures, very few asked questions as to the reasons why I behaved and expressed my feelings like I did. Because answers could not be determined, at least from their point of view, I believe that people decided to avoid the empathetic why questions, and instead focus on extinguishing those troublesome and mysterious behaviors. And so, when I was in third grade, it was determined that the "learning disabled" label no longer fit and that for special education purposes I was encoded as "emotionally disturbed" and sent to a special class at another school to have my behavior modified.

> Lunatic fringe on the edge of the shore
> A wave of untouchables floods the back door
> "Am I a label or merely a fable?
> Don't know who I am anymore."

Eventually, I would make it through college, and in the process of working with a social service agency obtain a diagnosis and medications that would soothe some of the mystery. Yet even today I confront the wonder and the horror of humanity. I struggle with the way in which I perseverate in ways that end up being hurtful in my relationships. I marvel just as strongly though at the stamina and endurance that come from the same perseveration, and internal vision. And as I do this I often hear Him say very gently to me, "It will kill you but you will love, one day you will know that it is not enough to stretch your tent of terror all around a tiny world, avoid the tumbling rough." Love of God and others is what He calls me to—not spiritual autism. And it is in that state of being that the internal and external worlds in me begin to converge.

Recently, I had another dream. In it a psychologist was seeking to map my soul in order to dissect it. He had a very literal understanding of my internal life—it is pathological and needed to be fixed. Without warning I was taken out to a swimming pool and placed in a group of professionals who were ready to baptize me by immersion. As I woke up I determined that I would cling to my identity as a child of God who adopted me through another water baptism long ago. A baptism into Himself. Into His broken Body which extended and was able to heal my world and bring me out of spiritual autism.

MYRIAM

Myriam is a student of pedagogy and psychology in Switzerland, where she was diagnosed by an Asperger's specialist in 2001. In the essay that follows, Myriam writes about her autistic traits and the ways in which they challenge her ability to communicate. Myriam believes that in order for effective teaching—let alone dialogue—to take place, "normal" people and those on the autistic spectrum must constantly ask one another for clarification and never assume that the other sees things the same way they do.

Myriam takes a practical approach in giving advice to professors and students, offering real solutions to common problems in pedagogy and communication.

My name is Myriam Huber. I am from Switzerland, 32 years old, and have Asperger's Syndrome. I am a student of pedagogics and psychology. I am interested in logic and language, psychology, physics, all kinds of encyclopedias, intellectually high gifted children and adults.

Connections between Pedagogics and an Autistic Brain

First of all there is a general question: Is it possible to discuss Asperger Syndrome/High-Functioning Autism in pedagogics? Or is it only discussable in education and development for individuals with special needs? I think not! Autistic people (and I am talking about high-functioning people with at least normal or above average intelligence) are predestined to join normal environments like parents-home, regular schools, regular colleges and universities. Although people with AS/HFA seem different to the nonautistic population (neurotypicals = NTs), they are capable of passing regular systems like anybody else.

If a problem comes up it is often not caused by the AS/HFA student, it is caused by the verbal and nonverbal answers of the environment, peers, parents, friends, the society. It *is* hard for NTs to understand the AS/HFA person indeed. The AS/HFA person seems to behave in a strange, not common way.

But if society and research label the AS/HFA personality as eccentric, egocentric, absorbed in their own world and not fitting in society, then this is only half the truth! An AS/HFA person can think of an NT as a strange person who does not do or say what she/he means, does not see all the peculiar microscopic visual differences around, cannot discriminate visual details and does not behave in a clear, logical way . . . and about NTs' thinking there is only one thing to say: "OUUUUUUUUUHHHHHHHHHHH . . ."

In my opinion the main difficulty in communication/interaction between AS/HFA and NTs is in the differences in thinking within an AS/HFA person and an NT.

Now I am trying to illustrate what I mean by different ways of thinking, but I am not sure if it is a frequent autistic problem or just one of many thinking-decoding problems of an AS/HFA person.

One sort of possible problem: I call it a kind of *theory-of-mind-problem* but at rather an advanced level.

From now on I am trying to make transparent what I am talking about while focusing on my own problems. Why focusing on my own problems? It is the only thing I know about . . .

My brain seems to be a very different brain which has problems finding connections to other people's brains. Why? I do not know. It was always that way and to find out why I would need the help of a so-called normal brain probably.

Possible Cases Which Cause
Communication/Interaction Problems:

Problem 1

Imagine person A and person B meet each other. They are looking up to the sky and watching clouds, both looking now at the same cloud and trying to see something special in it. Person A sees a rabbit-head in this cloud, person B sees a geometrical figure. Now person A thinks that person B sees the same thing and starts talking about the nutrition of animals. Person B also thinking that person A sees the same thing will be irritated because person B will think about angles, goniometric functions, 3-dimensional things . . .

Now transfer this situation to one where more than 99.9% of people mean the same as person A but you don't. You think B. And maybe even more than this: you are not only seeing a geometrical figure, but also a rabbit-head, a microscope, and a portrait of a male person. Now you are going to be irritated too, because you don't know what the rest of the people see in this cloud. A geometrical figure, a rabbit-head, a microscope, a portrait of a male person? You have no clue what is more probable. I will call this problem not a theory-of-mind-problem. I term it intellectual-egocentrism-problem.

Intellectual egocentrism in my opinion is the inability to know about other people's thinking. The inability to see what most other people see, the inability to think what most other people think . . . and I came to the conclusion that it is hardly possible to learn it some time. Am I wrong?

Problem 2

It is very difficult to understand multiple choices in a test. Is this sentence now meant in a logical way or is it meant in a colloquial way? In psychology I learned how multiple choice tasks inventors produce sentences which are wrong to distract the student.

Every time I have to solve multiple choice tests I am asking myself:

Is this sentence in this multiple choice a distractor and therefore it's wrong or should I identify it as wrong because it is not logical, or should I say it is right because most people in the world use it in this way, this colloquial way? I came to the conclusion that it is impossible to find out the answer to problems similar to this without asking back to the person who asked. It is the only way for me to understand how it is meant.

Problem 3

So-called open questions: you get a question to answer. Now there are two (A, B), three (A, B, C), or more (A, B, C, . . .) ways to understand how the question is meant and this will definitely influence your answer. Which one of the answers should you give? Answer based on "A," answer based on "B," or answer based on "C"? I am sure it is easier to answer the right way if you know the person well who poses the question. You know his/her use of grammatical rules, his/her logical quotient (for the concept of logical quotient see later). It would be easier if you could find out that a person who uses a special word or sentence over and over again always means only *one* special thing/content. Nevertheless it is almost impossible to know what is meant and you are forced to ask/inquire for more information; and sometimes there is no time to ask and you have to react without knowing more about it.

Surely, I do think that we understand each other most of the time without big problems. If we understand each other without problems then it is (in my opinion) because we immediately think the same or have the almost-same picture in our minds of what it could be or not and use (without really knowing) here a kind of "hidden logic" (= in my opinion a logic we use without really being aware of it) of what we mean. Without a minimum of logical rules we wouldn't understand anything . . . that also includes colloquial language. Colloquial language uses logic (logic rules) too.

About spoken language: I am not sure if spoken language is easier to understand than written language. Therefore a question to you AS/HFA person: Can you watch the whole person who talks, try to decode body language, nonverbal signals which will give you the reference and direction of the context of the topic the NT person is talking about? No, I think not. No, it is definitely not easier to understand because the person talking is using different voice frequencies and stresses words that do not seem to be important from my understanding. Or worse, I am distracted by this. Further, people do not seem to always stress the words the same way if they repeat the content later . . . and I am not able to know if it is meant as before or if it has a new meaning/aspect. An often exhausting procedure while interacting with persons. My brain is trying to decode most of the time. Then I feel like a computer whose understanding is totally dependent on logical tools.

I remember when I was at school: decoding language and its different meanings was a nice occupation to avoid boring school lessons, intellectually. Disadvantage: my intellectual egocentrism was unfortunately a thing I could not share with anyone. Until today. I am not sure if it is ever possible to find someone who understands this . . .

Here now a simple, rather stupid (but obvious) example how I decode spoken language: If the conductor in the train says: "All tickets please," then I immediately think, "What does all mean?" All MY tickets being in my purse? All tickets used for THIS special train? All tickets of ALL people on the train? Do I have to show them all? Do I have to show all of my tickets and one of the others'? Should everyone show his/her own tickets? Does he mean all tickets of traveling people in this railway compartment or of ALL compartments? No, not all compartments, because people traveling in another compartment aren't able to hear what the railway conductor is saying in our compartment. No, he does not mean all MY tickets when he needs only the one for this railway route. Every traveler has to show his/her ticket . . .

What do these examples have to do with pedagogy?

The answer is simple: If we want to discuss AS/HFA in pedagogics then it is necessary and urgent to talk about interaction and communication. And to discuss interaction and communication between AS/HFA persons and NTs it is required to talk about the AS/HFA's world of thinking.

How could it be possible to ever understand each other?

One way to decrease the problem of understanding communication is the use of *counterquestions.* It seems to be too simple, too trivial, to mention the importance of the counterquestion. Indeed, this aspect of communication seems so obvious, that a lot of people can forget. But: First, the counterquestion is the key for understanding. Second, it is one way to say to another person that she or he is interesting, is valued by thinking of her/him, is valued by asking more about her/his thinking and feeling. And this is definitely NOT a trivial aspect of communication.

To both of you, to the person with autism and the nonautistic person:

Ask counterquestions as much as needed if you want to know more about the inside view of another person's brain and feelings. If successful, this will give you answers to the other people's *logical quotient (LQ).* I do not think there is any great relation between people's LQ, but there is some hope that you can build logical-quotient-clusters between different persons. By the way, LQ is, unfortunately, not a very stable thing. It depends on the topic, the mood of the person, the surroundings, the analytical thinking level of a person. The higher the analytical level, the higher the logical quotient is. This is my own experience with rather logical and with rather illogical persons I got the opportunity to interact with.

What is the definition of logical quotient? It is predicated on the clearness of thinking, the logical use of words and sentences, the stableness of using it and the stableness of using it relative to time.

To the NT person:

Ask questions if you want to talk to the AS/HFA person. Ask as much as you need to understand the AS person.

To the AS/HFA person:

I think the only way to overcome your own intellectual egocentrism is to ASK the other person in the hope of understanding the meaning of the words this person puts together in a special context. A kind of "try to decode the NT's meanings of words and sentences with the assistance of the other person."

There exists an analogy between the computer-analyzer and the way to analyze as an autistic brain. But that is not all! There also exist your own feelings, biography, mood and context of feelings, mood and context of the other person's thinking.

Never forget that.

If pedagogics wants to understand the AS/HFA personality, it will have to overcome its pathological view of what we call "AS/HFA." Pedagogy should take it as a variant of living, thinking, feeling, and being. And should focus on the strength. As soon as this happens, AS and HFA will not only be a topic that has to be discussed, in psychiatry, special education, disability psychology. It will also take place in general pedagogics.

Models like SEM (Schoolwide Enrichment Model) of Prof. Joseph Renzulli and Prof. Sally Reis, University of Connecticut, USA, shows us that there is the possibility to integrate students of all different levels and styles of learning, thinking and being. Also Howard Gardner's concept of multiple intelligences gives us a new understanding of being and should be integrated in a new understanding of human being too.

And what about the problems? The learning style problems, the anxiety, the social problems, the perception problems, and the sensory problems of an AS/HFA person? They do exist, that is pretty clear. Anyway, a lot of these problems are *not* unknown in so-called normal children's education systems. It can happen to anyone, one time, one day, sometimes. Imagine an average, so-called normal student who is not willing to learn (no motivation) and has to do his exams. He is not able to answer the questions because he did not learn the required topic. He is not able to answer the exam questions because he is not able to understand the questions. He is not able to understand the questions because he is very frightened, cannot concentrate, and has a blackout. In my opinion these are similar feelings to those of an AS/HFA person.

The reason for having these feelings is different, but the outcome is similar (outcome is meant as outcome of feelings and outcome of exam grades).

People are not logical human beings, not easy to understand, and not always nice to interact with. Yes, but neither am I! And this probably irritates me most: How come I understand myself or seem to understand myself without bigger problems? Tell me if YOU know.

If there is anyone out there in the world who understands my problems of decoding other people's thinking and colloquial problems, let me know, please.

JIM

Though Jim was diagnosed with autism much earlier, his parents did not tell him until he was nineteen years old. He believes it is important to tell children as soon as they are diagnosed, as they already know that there is something very different about them.

The way that Jim dealt with his autism was to become, almost from birth, an anthropologist. Jim tells us that his need to study the "normal" culture in which he lived has made him an anthropology student unlike any other. Now, having been an anthropology student in the university, he cherishes his natural skills of observation, his patience in study, and his insatiable curiosity about Homo sapiens *as great gifts to himself, the university, and society.*

Jim believes that the emerging autistic culture provides a perfect place for him to serve as an autistic anthropologist.

I've been asked to write about my interest in anthropology and my experiences as an anthropology student, from the perspective of a college student with autism. I have what has been described as "high-functioning" autism because, while I meet the DSM-IV criteria for "autistic disorder," my IQ is higher than what is typically encountered in individuals with autism. According to my diagnostician I am excluded from a diagnosis of Asperger's Syndrome by my "history of slight delay in language usage, clinically significant delay in cognitive development and adaptive behavior."

I grew up in a small central-plains town in the United States. People were fairly conservative, and fairly accepting of natives of the community (but outsiders were and are considered "strange"). I've often wondered what people of my grandparents' generation thought of me as I was growing up. To some extent, I had a degree of security in that the people around me were inclined to accept my behavior. This allowed me to experiment with certain coping strategies in an atmosphere of security relative to that of many others with autism.

I was not told I was autistic until I was almost nineteen, and as far as I know, my school system was not told of the diagnosis either. This had a major effect on my childhood.

Autism, for me, is just the way things are. It means I don't receive and process information in the same manner as other people, not that I am stupid. It means I don't share the general neurotypical population's innate receptive and expressive communication skills; it doesn't mean I am unable to have feelings and emotions or am unable to share those emotions with others.

Let me give some examples here. As a child, I didn't understand the terms used to describe emotions. For the first seven years of my life, "happy" meant my blue toy truck. "Afraid" meant the *Wizard of Oz* poster on the wall of my bedroom that I was unable to ask to have removed; "sad" meant rainy weather. I didn't generalize that the emotion I felt when I was playing with my blue truck was the same as when my father came home.

Sometime—before I had a sense of time—I learned to read. I read the cards I received for my birthday. When I was five and six years old, I read the *Encyclopaedia Britannica* in hopes of understanding why I wasn't like everyone else. I read lots of interesting facts, but found no explanation.

When I was seven years old, on a visit to see a great-aunt, I discovered a collection of about fifty years of *National Geographic* in her basement. I spent most of the summer reading them. The articles described strange cultures and far-away lands in terms very similar to the way I thought about the world around me. That led me to the local library, where I found Ceram's *Gods, Graves, and Scholars*.

In the stacks near Ceram, I found works by Louis Leakey. An

examination of the bibliography led me to a whole new world. People actually wrote books about other cultures, and talked about how they studied them, what methods they used to understand them! I can remember thinking that the worlds they studied were as strange to them as the world around me was to me—so the same methodology should teach me about my world. This is the earliest generalization I can recall making; I was eight years old.

Many of the works dealing with evolution—human evolution—referenced works on animal behavior. This led me into ethology, and into that strange area where ethology and anthropology blend. Writers such as Robert Ardry, Robert Harding, and Jane Goodall led me even further afield. The most accessible writers of animal behavior for me were the hunters of Africa, so W. D. M. Bell and John Taylor joined my list of books to read.

Unfortunately, none of these books answered my questions. Some of the answers were there, but there was a vast contextual gulf between me and the information presented. I knew I was "different"; until then I didn't realize how different. That summer I was at least able to begin defining the difference and developing a structure to help me understand the society around me.

Rather broadly stated, I didn't think the same way as those around me. It's not as if I thought in another language—as best I can tell my thought processes were (and still are) different. I've never understood how others think, and aside from a few individuals I don't expect I ever will. That "contextual gulf" occurred because I simply couldn't understand the information in the manner in which it was presented.

In 1976, I read "The Flow of the River" by Loren Eiseley. It had no answers for me, but at last I had found someone who shared some of the same questions. I read a lot of work over the next year; something that has stayed in my mind were the words "Like the herd animals we are, we sniff at the strange among us." At nearly the same time, I read the works of Jack London and came away with the thought that among wolf-packs "to be different was to be dead." The closest analogy I had

at the time to the human behavior I observed around me was the behavior of wolf-packs; it was obvious to me I would have to change. It
was no longer enough to try to understand the society around me—I
had to learn how to no longer stand out, no longer be weird.

What was "weird"? Let me just say that at age ten I had a list of
several pages of areas of behavior where I differed substantially from
the norms I had identified around me. And I had no idea why. (Those
who know about my autism have asked me if I think children should
be told they are autistic. I have trouble understanding this—would you
ask someone if they thought a child should be told he or she is blind
or deaf? This is going to be a factor in the child's life *forever;* it seems to
me that to not tell her or him is at best neglectful. The trauma of knowing does not even approach the trauma of growing up not knowing
why the world is so difficult to comprehend.)

I considered a lot of approaches to dealing with the differences. I
had been recently introduced to the idea of "brainstorming"—just considering the question and writing down all possible answers, no matter
how improbable. I used a modified approach, in that I seemed unable
to consider an idea that was not practical to implement. Buying an
island retreat was financially impossible for me, for example.

The first Idea that came to mind was suicide. In retrospect, I can
understand the discomfort people have when they consider that a ten-
year-old boy actually did a cost/benefit analysis on suicide. (That wasn't
something that was a factor in my deliberations—I didn't understand
at the time that committing suicide would have an effect on others. Had
I known, I don't know if that would have been a factor.) One of the
positive benefits of suicide was that I would no longer have to deal with
a world I couldn't understand. It was outweighed by my curiosity about
the world around me.

The next possibility was to change myself to better fit into the society around me. Anyone who has ever dieted or tried to stop smok-
ing has an idea how difficult it is to institute permanent changes in
one's behavior—imagine changing literally everything about your

behavior, when you don't understand any of it. I actually tried to do this for about a year.

While I was busy trying to institute total permanent changes in my behavior, I developed an interest in lithic technology—stone tools. Writers spoke of "tool kits"; it seemed they were combining the physical technology and the cognitive skills under this single heading. I began to consider adapting this to my needs.

Such a "tool kit" would consist, for my purposes, of a package of cognitive skills and behaviors to meet the needs of a situation. This led me to task analysis. For example, in order to make coffee I need to: fill the reservoir on the coffee maker, put a filter in the basket, measure the coffee grounds, put the coffee grounds in the basket, put the basket in the coffee maker, place the coffee pot into place, and turn on the coffee maker. In situations calling for social interaction, a similar package or "module of behavior" would allow me to carry out social "tasks."

This was a real breakthrough for me, but it was obvious that it would take me forever to gain the skills and understanding I would need. I realized this after my first attempt at developing a behavior module failed miserably. My first attempt was at developing a module that would allow me to participate in recess activities with my peers.

I was playing basketball with my classmates at noon recess. Someone shot the ball but missed. I moved for the rebound. I was focused on the ball in typical autistic fashion, and injured one of the other players— I just ran him over. I didn't understand why the others were upset. By my understanding of "success" in this situation, I succeeded—I had recovered the ball for my team.

In study hall after lunch, I asked a classmate what I had done wrong. She said I should have apologized to the student I had injured. After a bit she said, "You don't understand—you really don't understand, do you?" (This was the first time any of my classmates directly asked me about my differences.) I didn't know what to say.

I told her what I was doing. She sat down and helped me develop what has evolved into the most successful of my behavior modules— ethics. Under this heading, we classified things that most would consider "manners." None of it made any sense to me, despite her attempts to explain, so we set some tentative rules and some default modes.

If I'm unsure how to behave, I can follow those rules. It may seem strange, but I won't be breaking any of the formal rules of society. I tend to be very polite with strangers, that way I won't offend people. Regardless of responsibility, I apologize. (I do realize that many people find these habits annoying, but I consider that better than to be seen as incredibly rude.)

I earlier alluded to the problem of a lack of experience and knowledge to develop these modules. Again, anthropology gave me the key. Stories and mythology have been used throughout history to transmit knowledge and cultural values to succeeding generations. If these, in company with those skills and values taught deliberately and by example, had proven adequate to prepare people for life as members of society, they should be of great assistance to me.

I began to consider "stories" as a means of gaining knowledge. Most legends and myths didn't seem particularly relevant to me as a member of 20th-century society (although *Beowulf* probably had more impact on me than almost anyone else in modern times). I went to the library and read the card catalog. Fiction seemed to be divided primarily into several genres so I selected a sample of each and began reading.

Do I need to point out that the "romance" genre was of no value to me? As best I could tell, it had no relevance to anything which had actually existed. "Detective stories" and "true crime" novels were of little use, although a few authors have become favorites. I enjoyed the intellectual challenge of solving the puzzle, and enjoyed competing against the protagonist, but most of what I read was, again, not relevant to my needs.

"Westerns" were fun in the same way that TV westerns were fun. It was nice to read something where I understood the rules and knew the good guy would always win. I quickly realized that the books were all written to a formula, and since this didn't provide the information I needed I abandoned the genre.

Improbably enough I settled on "science fiction" as the genre I was to use for a variety of reasons. (And before someone asks, no it wasn't because I identified with "Spock" on *Star Trek*. If with anyone in that TV series, I identified with "Engineer Scott" as he dealt with his engines and nothing else seemed to matter.)

Science fiction offered a number of things that made it attractive for my purposes. Ultimately, all science fiction deals with human interaction—the area in which I had identified serious deficits in my knowledge. I could clearly separate the fictional setting from the human interaction of the characters—something I was unable to do with most fiction and almost all television. As a friend once put it, I can say, "Everything I needed to learn about life I found in outer space." That isn't quite true, but I'm told it sounds funny.

"Funny." Anthropology, in all its myriad forms, has been of little help in understanding humor. As best as I can tell, humor is an interrupted defense mechanism. I say and do things that people find funny; they think I am making a joke when I am being totally serious.

Someone comes up to me and asks, "How are you doing?" Not so long ago I would have told them exactly how I was, including a statement of health and description of my recent activities. Now I reply, "I'm alive" and they think I'm trying to be funny. What they think of as "humorous" is an accurate statement of my state of being.

I've learned to deal with humor by observing the facial actions of the person telling the joke. If they are expecting a laugh in response, I laugh. It costs me nothing and I avoid being perceived as abnormal.

There are rules to humor. For instance, puns always call for a groan. Knock-knock jokes are often considered appropriate for children, and you can always respond with another. Limericks are frequently considered inappropriate for mixed company, as are most other forms of off-color humor. And never, ever, ask someone to explain a joke!

Anthropology hasn't explained lying either, but it has helped in some situations. I fail to understand why a person would deliberately misstate the truth, except when it serves to protect the person telling the lie. But under certain circumstances it serves as a social bonding mechanism. When someone shows you a newborn baby, they almost always say, "Isn't this a beautiful baby?" or some variation thereof. I used to tell the truth as I saw it; newborn babies are all rather ugly, but I could see why a parent would feel the baby has aesthetic value. What I didn't realize is the meaning of the question. When a person responds that a newborn is beautiful, they are also saying in essence that they accept the baby. At one time, this was very important as accepting the baby as a member of the group meant you were making a commitment to assist in the upbringing of the baby. So now, I just agree with the speaker.

Obviously, my "behavior modules" system had its shortcomings. I returned to the anthropological literature seeking answers. Someone, perhaps George Bird Grinnell, wrote that the stereotypical stoicism of Native Americans was their response to dealing with European culture. I needed to expand my behavioral modules concept to a "situational mask"—under most social circumstances I use certain behavior modules, but I needed to do something to ensure greater consistency in order that my behavior seem less abnormal.

Everyone does this. We behave differently in a job interview than in the bar on Saturday night. The difference is that I was going to have to do it deliberately, in all settings, and forever. (Right now there are two people with whom I do not feel the need to do this. With my best friend; I've never felt the need to hide anything—that's what best friends are for, right? One of my professors is also fully aware of my autism; judging by his reaction when I told him I no longer need to hide the autistic behaviors. I can in no way adequately describe the value to me of these two people.)

Having written a lot on the strategies I have developed, based largely on my studies of anthropology, it seems appropriate to end this essay by describing the success and failures of these strategies.

I was married for almost twelve years; the decision to seek a divorce was mine. Ultimately, I suppose the autism was a major factor, but others have suggested we just grew apart. For the first nine years of our marriage, my wife was unaware of the autism; after I told her it seemed like something changed. If we grew apart, that was the point it began; if there is any blame it is mine.

In my first attempt at college, I withdrew after less than a semester. I was unable to deal with the environment. Fluorescent lights, noisy equipment—noisy by my standards. Does anyone have any idea how painful it can be to listen to a microphone (when the professor doesn't operate it properly) dopplering in volume, let alone how impossible it is to process information presented in such a manner? A bad experience: Overhearing a conversation between two members of administration who had observed a man with autism shelving books in the library—one said, "Thank God we don't have any freaks like that here as students" and the other agreed with him. A worse experience? A teacher who frequently touched me.

Currently, I have been a full-time student for several years with a current GPA of 3.75 on a 4.0 scale. Functionally, it is incredibly stressful, but I manage. I am perceived as "strange" but in a university environment that isn't unusual. After I told my professor of the autism, he said he was considering suggesting that I be tested for ADD—and in a strange sort of way that is a success.

I work. I've been employed most of the time since I was about 14. I've learned to select jobs based on my strengths (I could never work in a fast food restaurant, for instance). Currently, by choice, I work a variety of part-time jobs that are scheduled around my classes and the times when I study best. Someday I will have a career as opposed to a job, and that is something that many people don't even consider for those with autism.

Emotionally, I get by. I realize that isn't very descriptive, but I am still working on correlating the vocabulary with the actual emotions. Most of the time I can pass as normal, when I am under stress people begin to notice I am not. If I am happy or excited, my body rocks and my voice changes but very few people know what this means.

If I am really stressed I try to escape to someplace safe, usually home. I live alone so no one is bothered if I pace for 36 hours. I get migraines very easily under these circumstances; this gives me an excuse that is accepted by almost everyone. As time goes on the times when I engage in self-injurious behavior grow farther and farther apart.

I realize my life is not what a lot of parents would want for their children, but it's a life. I have my studies, my work, and a few friends. I have a degree of satisfaction in life. It's important to remember that while my mind is different from the neurotypical population around me, it's my mind—and it's the only thing I know.

I've been asked many times if I could somehow be "cured" would I want to be. If I did that, I would no longer be me. I don't perceive anything wrong with what I am—the problem is with the way society relates to those like me. To ask if I would want to be "cured" is to suggest that my life now is somehow of less value. This is the way I was born, this is what I am. Would anyone suggest a member of any other minority seek a "cure"?

I'm a student of anthropology; in a manner of speaking I'm a student of the anthropology of autism. I'm one of the few who are in an inside position to observe and record the emerging "autistic culture." The Internet has brought many of us together in cyber-space, allowing us to learn from others whom we may never meet IRL—"in real life." The combination of our individual strengths can show us ways to do things that were considered impossible a generation ago. We are in the best position to understand ourselves, and to help each other regardless of our cognitive abilities.

These are exciting times to me as an autistic, and as an anthropologist. Not long ago my advisor told me, "Nothing made you an anthropologist, you were born an anthropologist." Most likely he will never realize the accuracy of his statement.

ANGIE

Angie has been tested as having "very superior" intelligence (even with a strong pattern of scatter in ability), and her ability to cope by sheer mental effort almost kept her from receiving a diagnosis of autism. She was, however, diagnosed when she began to have problems at university in Alberta, Canada. Her diagnosis was reconfirmed later by a professional in British Columbia. Angie illuminates the grinding pressure that most students with autism face, and how years of misunderstanding and lack of appropriate resources can lead to serious clinical depression at best, and to the total loss of a once energetic and promising individual at worst.

For university experiences, mine have been frankly disastrous. I've been 11 years in post-secondary school (10 in university) and have been in four different faculties. I have two bachelor degrees (that really are worth pissing on—sorry for the vulgarity) and have once again, hit the wall in graduate school. The wall was in fact an entire department who, for all reasons I can see, have teamed up against me once they mutually decided I can be a bit too much trouble. I have voluntarily withdrawn (and am technically on medical leave), and have pretty much reached the point where I pretty well refuse just about any contact from anybody for any reason. I just don't need to be told yet again how inadequate I am. Although I have worked in the past successfully as a secretary (however not without a ridiculous amount of agony initially), I am embarrassed to work at this anymore because of the sheer length of time I have devoted to becoming something more. If I have to resort to working as a receptionist (or anything else that involves direct contact with people) at this point I'd rather take pills.

As for DX, mine is Asperger's. Just too many things have happened while I was growing up as well as troubles I still have today for *anyone* not to be convinced.

As well, I know it is hard to diagnose in adulthood because we can learn to compensate and cover. At the same time, though, there is also a significant post-traumatic component as I was an abused child (psychological, physical, and sexual abuse) and have not been in contact with my family for years. I am responding to school, especially the last few years in grad school, like it was yet another traumatic event in my life, complete with chronic nightmares and extreme aversion to any situations that look like what I was doing in school (Speech Pathology). I am frightened to be put into a situation where I have to explain anything to anyone (unless of course I can write it down, go off and stew about it on my own time), any situation where someone is closely monitoring my behaviors and anything that requires me to speak competently. To some extent I may have a genuine difficulty picking out appropriate details and my verbal memory is also relatively weak as well. I also have great frustrations with not properly recalling right words when I do try to talk and often feel like an idiot. I remember surprisingly little of what people tell me, especially when there are names involved. Much of my anxiety may simply be due to my being sick of having my nose rubbed in it with no one being gracious or respectful enough to tell me just what the hell I was expected to do or what was implied.

What I sometimes do get frustrated about is downright cognitive dissonance and limited thinking. Most of the time I just keep it to myself because I just make too many enemies when I say something. I only do what seems right and reasonable.

In terms of this anthology, I'm not sure if you'd want me in the anthology because clearly nothing in my life has worked in the most global sense. I have been broken many times, probably attributable to some extent to AS, and this time I'm not really sure if I have anything in me to recover and, as a consequence, can't offer any useful advice. I do very little that's productive during my days and don't really want to anymore, living on welfare and stringing a few beads on the beach for minimal money. I have no dreams or aspirations anymore, and usually like it best when I can be left alone. I am not really interested in anything anymore (although I once had the remarkable ability to be interested in anything). In fact, I truly wish I had mental retardation instead because most people get what the hell that is and my life probably would have turned out better. I am perfectly happy just to tell people that I am in fact retarded, which is not hard to do if you can't remember the right words in the first place, remember people's names, hear well against noisy backgrounds, clue in to important details that everyone else gets, etc. . . . I just don't think anything I have to tell would really help anyone with AS cope in life. If anything, I'm exactly what a person would NOT want to be.

ARTHUR

Arthur has a B.A. in anthropology and was diagnosed with an Autism Spectrum Disorder at the University of California (Los Angeles) Medical Center in 1996 at the age of twenty-three. His short essay reveals that apart from his academic concerns, he has, like his neurotypical peers, a very present concern about attracting intimate partners. Though this was not expressed as a concern for any other of the essayists, social interaction between the sexes is a very important part of the "normal" university/college student's experience (some might argue it is the dominant one, taking precedence over studies). Arthur's reflections are valuable because they seem to be rare.

I was sort of drawn to anthropology because it let me explore different cultures and different kinds of people. I've always been fascinated by the difference in how people speak, worship, dress, etc. And anthropology seems to focus on that. It's amazing how many different kinds of cultures and lifestyles there are in this world. I always liked archaeology too because it dealt with discovering and exploring things. My only regret about my major is I wish I had devoted more time to archaeology.

I'm sensitive to dry stuff such as walking barefoot on the dry sand. I don't like it when my hands are dry. Of course my main fear is approaching people and talking to people of the opposite sex. My experiences with women much to my dismay are limited. Unfortunately I have not met anyone who is willing to be patient with my inability to spontaneously communicate. I know that I'm an attractive, intelligent male; however, I lack the ability and courage to go out there and find someone. It is like being an artist with a rubber brush standing in front of an empty canvas. I am open to any suggestions you may have. When you have so few experiences rejection hits hard. Not wanting to scare anyone away I retreat very quickly and basically give up. I don't know how to play the game as I see and speak things as I see it. I guess you might say I have many autistic moments where I say exactly what is on my mind. Humor is hard for me to understand when you take things literally. It's so difficult when you see the world as it is but you don't really feel a part of it. I feel confident that if the right person gave me a chance they would discover a world of unexplored treasures.

I would like people to understand that autism doesn't equal stupidity. If I say I'm autistic people will probably think I'm mentally retarded in some kind of way when in fact I'm just as smart or even smarter than most people. I don't think people see my potential because I'm not good at communicating socially. It's harder to find a job when you can't communicate as well as other people.

CHRIS MARSH

Chris, diagnosed with autism both in 1997 (age twenty-six) at Marshall University's psychology clinic and again in 1998 through the Maryland Department of Rehabilitation Services, expresses his belief that matching ASD people's skills with their university training is crucial. Employment worries after training, like those Arthur expresses in his essay, are shared by many people with Autism Spectrum Disorders. In this letter to the disability coordinator of his alma mater, Chris explores concerns we have about finding satisfying employment after university.

I am concerned for some future college students who have disabilities such as Asperger's Syndrome. Their transition into traditional roles such as employment may be very problematic. A freshman, whether disabled or not, at college may not realize that there is more to preparing his/her future than keeping a high GPA.

College is a secure place where on-campus students have housing and food if not also parental health insurance. It can also be a very pleasurable place with the Internet, cable TV, video games, a variety of activities, football games, etc. For many students, reality seems distorted. Most traditional college students have never had to work for a living yet. Many have never known hunger, homelessness, or poverty.

For example, my Mom and Dad worked hard, saved, sacrificed, and struggled for years before they bought a West Virginia country home and I was born. I lived through only their best career years. Many children of successful parents do. What I also didn't know until grad school was that, because of history, demography, and discrimination, my parents' birth cohort (1930s decade) experienced far greater returns from their 1950s-era college educations!

If the college is full of Ph.D.s, it should not imply that every Ph.D. gets a high-status, if not also high-paying, job. Heck, I thought my first professors were rich. In America, everything essential to life costs money. Money is earned through employment, as skills developed in college create a profit for an employer. Parents certainly do not live forever and few live longer than their adult children. Whether or not colleges are raising tuition faster than the rate of inflation, the current financial aid system puts the entire burden of payment and repayment almost entirely on students and/or parents. It is said that education is never wasted even if one studies the wrong major, but one spends time and money and dreams that can never be replaced. One may have student loans as a result. One may also be dissatisfied with and overeducated for employment that does exist. One may also offend one's future managers, who may be less educated. But I was wrong to believe that my liberal arts degree would be as equally and as immediately valuable as those of my parents. My disability made my job transition difficult and financially/emotionally painful. Asperger's Syndrome is an excellent example of a disability that poses an occupational handicap but not an academic one. If others with Asperger's apply they could face my problems, too.

Without too many details, after grad school, I interviewed frequently, presumably on the facts conveyed in my resume. However, presumably because of poor presentation management and unfavorable competition with other sociology majors, I was only selected for a temporary federal position which I could not complete successfully. My failure to secure credential-appropriate employment forced me to settle, grudgingly, for employment appropriate for my high school diploma or middle school certificate. The fact that the skills of most of the population are satisfactory for these mostly temporary industrial labor jobs meant that I was low-paid. What this meant was that I qualified for, and received, social supports such as food stamps, Medicaid, unemployment compensation, and rehabilitation. I also had to live with my mother because I was not paid enough to get my own food, housing, car, and medical care and repay my student loan, which was deferred. Finally, the absence of health insurance coverage made my cancer, a medical problem, a financial one. Fortunately, with most of the debt cancelled for insolvency, I paid off the remaining bills in two years. The only debt I still have is my student loan from graduate school. College students, especially those with disabilities, have worse things to worry about than fitting into their peer group and dating. This is not to say that these things are not important, however, nor that they are harder for students with disabilities. But even with college credentials, many may fail in the work world.

Any college student with a known disability or special education experience should, in my opinion, contact a career counseling official before making a decision on a college major, and the sooner the better once coming to college. Career counseling can work. I know it can, because the State of Maryland "backed up" and did my career assessment over from scratch. After a re-diagnosis of my disability, including an IQ test, and consultation with a career psychologist, I passed entrance tests at a state vocational rehabilitation facility. I earned straight As in college-level courses and have been stably employed since shortly after graduation.

The only question I have is, if Maryland did it, why can't a college do it? Why shouldn't a college? I hope you do not take this question personally or negatively, but I believe career mistakes, even mine, are preventable. Students need to know what lies ahead, what's at stake, so they can ask for advice. I don't think sociology was an absolute mistake: it did teach me about social issues such as conformity, socialization, interaction, and so on (Emile Durkheim) that are helpful in my rehabilitation. But my social research career was an occupational mistake. It cost me over $70,000, society $25,000, and my widowed mother several thousand dollars.

What really hurt, however, was being rejected for the job role I yearned to fill. I was labeled by peers as mentally retarded when I was younger. During some of my temp jobs, I felt retarded. I also felt betrayed when the State of Maryland wanted to spend state money to train me in something else. I was not prepared for society, as my department aspires to achieve.

I want to help other college students or graduates.

DOUGLAS O'NEAL

Douglas O'Neal, age thirty-two, teaches astronomy and physics at a small college. He earned a Ph.D. in Astronomy and Astrophysics from Pennsylvania State University. He has been interested in astronomy since childhood —one case of an obsessive youthful interest becoming a lifelong passion. He's one of three brothers, and grew up in the Charleston, West Virginia, area.

Interests outside of work include the outdoors, classical music, creative writing, nonfiction reading, and sports.

The mental health professionals Doug has seen since he first heard of Asperger's Syndrome two years ago agree that he has this disorder. Looking back, he believes that this diagnosis makes sense of his university experiences.

I sit on a park bench beside the Henderson mall, gazing up at the canopy nearly closed by the lush green of four giant, stately elms. This path, this tunnel through the trees, is my sacred grove. On this breezy summer day, a wispy sky and dapples of sunlight striking the grass beneath the elms, sweet memories of years spent living, learning in this place, I wonder—can there possibly be any more beautiful place on Earth? This is my place of comfort and power and spiritual rest—this is my home. This is Penn State.

I lived and studied there for ten years, receiving a bachelor's degree in 1990 and a Ph.D. in 1997, both in Astronomy and Astrophysics. I love

the place, and nowhere in the world is more special to me or more significant in my life. People who get to know me have no doubt that I'm
a loyal Penn Stater. My collection of Penn State souvenirs proves that: at
last count, it includes seven t-shirts and four sweatshirts and miscella-
neous other articles of clothing; and many other items from key chains
to refrigerator magnets, from a mouse pad to a Joe Paterno bean bag
buddy.

With my August 1997 Ph.D. graduation, I've passed firmly into
alumni-hood. My heart will always bleed blue and white, for not only
was Penn State the university where I gained an education—it was
also the place where I lived during the decade that determined much
about who I am and my course in life. During my years in the aptly
nicknamed Happy Valley (it's actually called Nittany Valley, hence Nittany Lions), I came to love the mountain ridges and their hiking trails,
the lush forests of that Appalachian land, and a town neither too big nor
too small, neither too isolated nor too urban, that gradually over the
course of the years came to be my home in the most important sense.

Thinking less idealistically, Penn State was also my university—
where I was first exposed to a diversity of American and international
culture, where I learned the essentials of my chosen field of study,
where I learned how to be a scientist by doing significant, original research. I had many good teachers there, and some bad ones too. I am
grateful to the good ones, and with few exceptions, I harbor no malice
toward the bad ones.

Yet, as much as I love the place, whenever I set foot on the Penn
State campus, so many bad memories that live there come back to me
too. Despite the thousands of people around, I had many more social
failures than successes. Memories of my time as an undergraduate
often involve spending Friday and Saturday evenings alone, having
nothing to do, no friends who were thoughtful enough to invite me to
join them for some activity. I tried, but largely failed, to fit into at least
three different social groups. Despite the fact that I lived in Atherton
Hall, home of many students in the University Scholars Program, I

found little fellowship. My study habits, perhaps, didn't help matters. School was easy for me, and I would get all my work and studying done before others. Thus I had no use for study groups, and I could not sympathize with those who had to pull all-nighters the night before a test was given or a homework set was due. Looking back on those years, I know that, due to the way I was raised, I was not very mature and, in general, ill-prepared to adapt to the social style of even the "nerdy" among college students—but at the time, it was painful and lonely. It almost goes without saying that my dating experiences as an undergraduate were essentially nonexistent.

For the most part, it was little better when I became a grad student. Again, school was easier for me than it seemed to be for most of my grad student colleagues. In a hard science department, I guess I was a "nerd among nerds"—as sorry as that sounds. Nowadays, it seems that when other recent departmental graduates return to State College for a visit, the students and perhaps faculty who remain take them out for a meal or throw them a party. I've been back many times since my graduation—no free dinners, no parties. Of course, the social style of most of my colleagues was markedly different from mine. For most of the grad students, being "social" meant "let's go to a bar where we can hardly hear each other and talk about movies and pop music!" A party meant "let's get really drunk and talk about how evil our professors are!" Fine if you're into that sort of stuff, but I'm not, never have been, probably never will be. If I held a party I'd be lucky to get two or three of my fellow students there—because the rest of them weren't interested if it wasn't going to feature alcohol and loud music. At the time I could rationalize these things, but that didn't prevent me from experiencing, way too often, sharp feelings of rejection.

Sometimes when I'm at Penn State, I see things—the dorm I lived in as an undergraduate, a shop I used to frequent in the evenings—that remind me of past times. Amidst the nostalgia, unpleasant memories also live there, the isolation and rejection that I felt in my then-still-immature soul. When I remember such lonely times, the beauty of the crystal blue sky and the living green landscape seems to take on a painful aspect, seems to be telling a lie. When I walk into the restaurant that I visited with a spiritual/social student organization I helped start, just before it all blew up, and recall how much of my heart and soul I put into it only to have it come back and bite me in the ass, I think that I would not want to relive my student days. When I remember all the nights I wished for someone, anyone to spend time with, I'm sure I wouldn't—unless somehow, magically, I could transfer to my younger self the things I now know about myself and the world.

I also got in some arguments, most of them over minor issues, with various members of the department. In retrospect, I take responsibility for most of these, and in no small part they came out of the long-term depression I describe below. Despite this, most if not all of the faculty of the Astronomy and Astrophysics department remained highly supportive of me throughout my time there; I particularly thank Drs. Eric Feigelson and Jim Neff, respectively my undergraduate and graduate advisors. (Jim now teaches at the College of Charleston, South Carolina.)

For several years, including all of my time in grad school, I was clinically depressed. My social difficulties were almost certainly both a cause and an effect of this. I only started getting treatment in the autumn of the last of my ten academic years at Penn State; I only started taking anti-depressant drugs one year after I finished grad school. Since then, I've realized some important things about why I seldom fit in socially—including a probable diagnosis of Asperger's Syndrome, a high-functioning autism that causes me to have a different social style and different preferences than most people. Since grad school I've become more confident in social and interpersonal situations. I've also grown in other ways, including finding a new spiritual community (the Unitarian-Universalists), and finding several great new friends.

I would not feel the way I do about Penn State if all my experiences there had been bad. It was there that I gained an appreciation for the outdoors and came to enjoy hiking. I had some good social and recre-

ational contacts through the Quiz Bowl team and the Penn State Astronomy Club, and both these organizations gave me friendships that
still persist. I fondly remember the long car rides to quiz bowl tourna-
ments, nerdy conversations about any imaginable topic; I remember
looking forward to the weekly practice sessions, a chance to forget my
other concerns and engage for a couple hours in friendly academic
competition. With the Astronomy Club, I remember all the open
houses on the roof of Davey Lab, showing visitors the celestial sights
and then taking a moment to peer out over the wall, gazing upon campus and town from above and at the lovely ridges beyond. I remember
the out-of-town observing trips, nights spent in fellowship under the
stars, squeezing the 10-inch Dobsonian telescope into my trunk and
driving to a place where the sky's beauty is unfettered by the lights of
town. I remember returning to State College late at night and dinner
in the wee hours at 24-hour restaurants. Those are fond memories of
my years at Penn State.

Early in my time in grad school, mostly through the influence of
my friend Alex Richman, I started following certain non-football Penn
State sports. I'm still an avid fan of the women's volleyball team. It
helped that we had joined the Big Ten Conference, leaving the Atlantic
10+/-2 far behind. It's quite a bit more interesting, more "sexy," when
your big conference matches are against Ohio State, Wisconsin, and
Michigan, than when they're against St. Bonaventure, Duquesne, and
Rhode Island.

In summary, considering the good as well as the bad, I changed and
matured immensely during my time at Penn State. During my senior
year (undergraduate, in 1990), I was considering where to go for graduate school, and I chose Cornell University. I didn't last long. What I really wanted was to return to Penn State. Starting a Ph.D. program in
astrophysics is itself a daunting task.

Combining that with adjusting to a new university and a new
town, and moving farther from home, was at that time in my life more
than my psyche could handle. All in all, I'm glad I made that choice.

The "Cornell thing" was by no means good. But as Dr. Pangloss sings in Bernstein's *Candide*, "Sweet honey comes from bees that sting," the best of results from the worst of circumstances: the year away from school allowed me to pursue some other interests (including creative writing) and thus to begin an important part of my maturation. I quickly left Ithaca and returned to my family in Hurricane, West Virginia, for the remainder of the 1990–91 academic year. No, I would not want to go back to my younger, student days. But I do go back there and visit, and when I'm there, I do things I did when I was a student— volleyball, quiz bowl, astronomy. I still visit friends there, and occasionally make new ones. But the deepest, most essential reason I return to Penn State is for individual and personal things: for the wooded mountain ridges, for the sweet breezes in the elms, for the calling of home.

Sometimes it is almost disconcerting to me how familiar I am with Penn State. It's almost as if I know every building, every lawn, every tree and sidewalk crack on campus. Penn State gave me many things. The most special thing I can say about Penn State is—it is my true home. That is why I love it, that is why I go back there. Blessed be that place forever in my heart.

SUSAN

Susan is a thirty-year-old graduate student in linguistics at a prominent American university. She was born in 1970 in Los Angeles, California, and passed many of her early developmental milestones without problems (such as crawling at six months and walking on her first birthday), but she was also an unusually silent baby and rarely cried except at mealtimes.

She began to manifest typical autistic behaviors by age one; these included a general lack of interest in people and surroundings, absorption in various visual stimuli such as candles and spinning toys, frequent twirling of fingers near the eyes, and play limited to the manipulation of objects like belt buckles for hours. Her spoken vocabulary was limited to four words and she was functionally nonverbal until she was four years old. Her parents suspected she had hearing problems, but tests on four separate occasions showed this not to be the case. At age four she was certified LD (learning disabled) after tests showed marked deficiencies in auditory memory and motor ability, and she was enrolled in special education at a school for disabled children. However, the tests did not support a specific diagnosis.

In high school her social problems had subsided somewhat as she found her place in a group of "nerds and geeks," where conversation tended to revolve around Star Trek and intellectual topics. Academically her performance was only average (grades were largely Bs, Cs, and Ds), as she rarely found schoolwork as inspiring as her private interests. Socially she found little reason to attend most high school functions and in particular she found pep rallies to be both irritating and stupid. Although she did not think much about college, she applied at the last minute and began attending her local university in 1988. She has subsequently received bachelor's and master's degrees in linguistics and hopes to complete her Ph.D. in several years. She was diagnosed with Asperger's Syndrome last year at Stanford University.

Her essay is a revealing look at the ways that autistic people experience the world radically differently than those around them.

The only thing I've wanted to do with my life is to research. When I was in high school, I tried to think of a career well suited to my abilities. I had toyed with the idea of being a freelance writer as I liked the independence and solitude it would bring, but I knew I would not fare well in the realm of fiction. I had rarely read fiction myself since it was quite difficult for me to imagine different characters and personalities, even in the science fiction and fantasy genres. I would easily get lost in the first third of a book. I was much more interested in writing about things that happened or describing scenes and places in exquisite detail. As a result, most of the reading I had done up to that point was nonfiction and dealt with either history or science.

I ultimately gave up the idea of being a freelance writer because I was more interested in researching than writing. I realized that while I may still publish the results of my research, the profits from such work would not be enough to live on. I came to this conclusion only indirectly since I did not think too far ahead about my future. When I graduated from high school, the only thing that was on my mind at the time was Charles Manson. I had just read Bugliosi's *Helter Skelter* and I was in the process of constructing a long timeline of all the events associated with the activities of the Manson Family. I wanted to catalogue every piece of information about the murders and trial. As far as I was concerned, I would have been happy to do this as long as it took. I was living at home and such a drastic change as going to college did not seem important. With high school now out of the way, I had all the time I wanted to pursue my interests.

Upon the urging of my parents, I had already taken the SAT and sent in my application to the local university. But college was nowhere in my consciousness. However, by summer's end, I had completed my study of the Manson Family and one of my older interests, linguistics, was revitalized. And fortunately for me, linguistics courses were being offered at the university. This presented me an irresistible opportunity to research my favorite interest.

Linguistics actually perpetuates one of my oldest interests. I had a hyperlexic fascination with written language as early as age 2. At this time, my spoken language consisted of just four words: *mima* 'mother,' *dida* 'father,' *shuga* 'water,' *baka* 'milk.' These words were only used instrumentally, to get the attention of my parents and to get them to do things for me, such as the giving of water or milk. My language delay persisted for some time. When I was 4 and 5 years old, my mother and I often communicated with pictures and drawings. I also had much difficulty responding to open-ended questions such as "What do you want to eat?" and my mother had to ask yes-no questions, "Do you want x, y, z, etc." until she guessed the right answer. I finally began to speak in sentences when I was 4½ years old, but with mixed-up word order. My mother recalls an example: "Outside by go train the." I did not speak fairly normally (except for a persistent lisp) until I was 7. But I still had a lot of lingering problems with the nuances and idioms of English.

But despite these struggles with spoken language, I had long been fascinated by written language. My mother tells me that my favorite "toy" at age 3 was the dictionary, and I would spend hours each day poring through its pages. One of the first things that attracted me was the shape of the letters. There were straight lines and curves, bulges, and dots. There was repetition of the same letters over and over again in a text. But the most attractive feature of written language is the intense color. I experience synesthesia, which is a form of cross-sensory perception, enabling me to perceive music in color and certain shapes (like numbers and alphabet letters) in color. This adds immensely to my enjoyment of music and reading.

My favorite colors are bright colors such as green, red, and blue, while I find yellows, oranges, browns, purple, and black to be quite irritating. With varying shades, my green letters are "g," "h," "l," "p," "w," my red letters are "b," "k," and "m," and my blue letters are "n" and "s." These letters are very pretty to me. I also like the freshly green number "2," the aquamarine blue "5," and the bloody red "8." The more dull letters are the yellow "c," "f," "y," and "u," the orangish "q," light brown "d," and reddish brown "t." I very much dislike the purple "v," the black "j," "e," "r," "z," and the strange polka-dotted "x." As far as numbers are concerned, most are drab or ugly like the dark brown "4," the sickly orange "6," the black "7," and the plain yellow "9." But I would rather experience these dull and ugly letters than not see any colors at all.

As I spent my days going through the dictionary and learning gradually about the world, these colors made intuitive sense to me. They were linked into an idiosyncratic semantic system I was developing about the letters, in which letters denoted not phonetic elements but entire worlds of meaning. Let me cite a few examples. The letter "C" iconically resembles the "C"rescent moon and it has the shimmery yellow color of the moon. And as Cookie Monster points out in his "C is for Cookie" song, a "C"ookie may be munched to a crescent moon-like shape. The letter therefore embodies the mysterious "C"elestial qualities of the moon and this theme was developed in several dreams I clearly recall from my early childhood. But "C" is not only celestial, it is also richly fancy, decorated, and ornate. This impression was gained by the pictures and definitions in the dictionary of such words as cabriole, cabriolet, candelabrum, capitals, cathedral, cello, ceremony, chaise, champagne, chandelier, chasuble, chauffeur, cinquefoil, ciborum, cittern, clerestory, cloister, coach, coat of arms, coffers, column, commode, coronet, cross, crown, and so forth. The letter "T" resembles both a "T"elephone pole and a "T"ree and therefore has the reddish brown color of wood. The image of a telephone pole also links into streetside scenes of trucks, trains, trolleys, traffic, and tires. The letter "S" for me evokes water and links into all the words starting with "s" that deal with the ocean (sea, sand, shore, ship, sampan, sloop, schooner, scull, sailor, sailboat, starfish, seal, squid, shrimp, swordfish, sturgeon, sperm whale, surf, sink, swim, etc.), taking a bath (shower, soak, soap, shampoo), and inclement weather (storm, splash, snow, sleet).

This hyperlexic interpretation of written language remains intact in my mind, though I have long since adopted more conventional approaches to the printed word. However, my synesthesia has made the study of language an intriguing sensory experience and it has always lingered somewhere in the background. In seventh grade I tried to learn German and I enjoyed it partly because of the icy coolness I perceived in its words. Then in eighth grade I became completely fascinated by the "so-and-so begat so-and-so" lists of Genesis, chapter 10 and I attempted to research the etymology of each name. Some names were very beautiful like Peleg and others were rather hideous like Arpachshad. At the same time I was interested in the Sumerian and Egyptian king lists and found much to enjoy in names like Weneg (a second Dynasty king of Egypt) and Gilgamesh (a king of Uruk).

Once I entered high school, this interest in etymology evolved into an obsession about linguistics. I discovered the discipline of historical linguistics, the primary activity of which is the reconstruction of ancient protolanguages through the careful comparison of cognates in descendant languages. Differences between languages are usually very regular and sound correspondences between the languages allow historical linguistics to reconstruct what the parent protolanguage was like. I found the regularity of the sound correspondences to be very satisfying. For instance, one famous correspondence laid out in Grimm's Law specifies that Germanic *f* corresponds to Latin *p* (i.e., English *father*, Latin *pater*), Germanic *th* corresponds to Latin *t* (i.e., English *three*, Latin *tres*), and Germanic *h* corresponds to Latin *c* (i.e., English *horn*, Latin *cornu*). This correspondence holds up over thousands of words and I enjoyed seeing the same thing happen over and over again. But there was also a synesthetic element to my interest as well. Many of the reconstructed Proto-Indo-European words looked very pretty to me, abounding in greenish letters like *sneigwh* 'snow,' *gwei* 'live,' and *dhwer* 'door.'

I spent many high school recesses and afternoons in the school library, poring through dictionaries and collecting every Indo-European cognate I could find. I compiled my research into cognate lists for each Proto-Indo-European root and I was never seen at school without my manila folders stuffed with notes. By the time I started college, I had memorized hundreds of Indo-European and Austronesian cognate sets. I took an introductory linguistics course in my first semester and very quickly I knew I wanted to pursue linguistics as a career.

However, as much as I loved comparative historical linguistics, I eventually abandoned it in favor of research on nonstandard varieties of English in the 19th and 20th centuries. My research was highly original and innovative. For six years I exhaustively looked through all the criminal court records at the State Archives, old newspapers on microfilm, school newspapers and yearbooks, diaries—almost any available text I could find for the relevant period that contains attestations of nonstandard speech. My database currently prints out to 800 pages single-spaced in tiny font. This research has led to numerous research publications in my field and contributed to theories on language change. It also gave me the opportunity to explore one of my other early childhood obsessions: architecture. I became obsessed with the history of the buildings in the downtown area and while I researched archival records for information on language use, I also took notes on the construction and demolition of buildings, fires, or any other relevant information. I also attempted to collect every available photograph of the downtown area over the past 200 years. I eventually memorized the construction and demolition dates of hundreds of buildings and developed the ability the visualize what any place downtown looked like since 1850.

These activities kept me very busy. My interests all seemed to involve the theme of historical change and perhaps their appeal lies in their potential in helping me understand change in my own personal life. Fortunately, my undergraduate experience in college was not as traumatic as it could have been. I went to the local university in town and continued to live at home with my parents for most of my undergraduate years. I do not think I would have been prepared to face the demands and challenges of dorm life or living in an apartment off campus. Going to college was much like going to another high school, except now I got to spend more time studying what I liked and I faced fewer social demands. There were no more pep rallies, cliques, and bullies, and unlike most people, I did not think of college as a place to make friends, go to parties, and so forth. It was just a place to study. So in a large part, the change initially was small and for the better. It would have been a lot different if I had gone away to college.

There were still problems. Initially I had a difficult time orienting myself to the new campus and I kept getting lost. The university presented me with a wealth of new sensory experiences to get accustomed to, and the environment occasionally taxed my energy and patience. It seemed to be more crowded than high school and registration day, when seemingly the entire student body squeezed itself into tiny Building 17, was particularly hellish. I was rarely seen walking on campus without simultaneously reading or listening to my headphones. For some reason, such distractions were comforting. My walkman was also a social buffer, as I routinely listened to music between classes and while I was in the library or the linguistics department—situations which potentially involved social interaction. I don't think I intentionally strove to avoid people; it was more a matter of comfort.

I did have two friends during this period. One was a boy I knew from high school who caught the same bus in the morning to the university, and typically I talked to him at length (and fairly exclusively) about whatever I was researching at the moment, whether it was linguistics, religious history, or Yardbirds music. Another was a girl from another high school who had become my best friend. We talked on the phone every night at 9 P.M., met at libraries and the local shopping center with her aunt and uncle, and communicated frequently via letter. She had a profound influence on me and she helped me learn countless social skills. One example stands very clearly in my mind. We were in the back of her aunt's car and she gave me a Chick-o-Stick candy. I took it without saying anything and put it away. Annoyed and upset, she demanded to know why I didn't say anything. I insisted that I felt very appreciative and thought it was obvious to her that I was, though I did not think to say anything verbally. She could not understand how I could possibly think that, and not knowing anything about Asperger's Syndrome, I had no way of explaining how I assumed that she could read my mind. Because of this frustrating incident, I made a mental note to always say "thank you" when given something. I also studied her intently in the nine years I knew her and extensively modified my mode of self-expression in the process. Many of my expressions, from the patterns of intonation in my voice to the way I smile, have existed only since my early 20s and were copied directly from her. My current boyfriend sometimes tells me that despite my awkwardness and shyness I seem to express myself naturally, but I know it comes only with great effort and sometimes strain.

Tuition was fairly cheap at $800 a semester but I had to earn most of the money myself. I found work at a small university library and though the pay initially was minimum wage, it was a job that I found to be quite enjoyable. The first task of the day was always shelving books that patrons had used, and I liked putting the books into call number order and then finding the places they belonged on the shelves. The next task would usually be checking in the new journals that had arrived in the mail. I would stamp each journal with two different stamps and then record the issue number and date of receipt into the Kardex file. I enjoyed keeping track of the dates and predicting when a journal would arrive or watching to see if it was delayed compared to the year before or *vis-à-vis* the patterns over the prior ten or twenty years. Several years later, the library became automatized and the old card catalogue was rendered obsolete; I was worried that my precious

Kardex file was also in danger of becoming outmoded. I begged my boss to not get rid of it, and as far as I know it is still in use. I was a rather slow worker, easily spending an hour checking several journals into the Kardex for instance, but this did not bother my boss much. She told me she appreciated my precision, carefulness, and honesty. One of my workmates however took notice of my literal-mindedness and found me to be quite amusing, teasing me whenever I misunderstood something he said. He told me on several occasions that talking with me was like engaging in a "Who's on First" routine, an allusion to the Abbott & Costello sketch in which an individual misconstrues the names of people as words.

I soon discovered that my language difficulties also began to affect my academic work. Although I had taken two years of French in high school and a year in college, the Conversational French class was torturous. I simply could not process language in real time, and I could not overcome the obstacle of thinking in English. The following semester I enrolled in The Structure of French, a course that was taught entirely in French. I walked out of the classroom on the first day without understanding hardly a single word. But reading French was not difficult at all. I therefore decided to focus on languages that involved only visual input. I took classes in Greek and Latin for two years and found them to be quite easy, as they focused on the translation of texts into English. I even briefly contemplated switching my major to Classics. I also excelled in areas of linguistics that emphasized visual input, such as syntax, which represented sentence structure in tree diagrams, and textual analysis. On the other hand, I found the classes in phonology and phonetics to be frustrating, though not as difficult as semantics and pragmatics proved to be. The notions that lay behind such terms as conversational implicature, entailment, and illocutionary acts seemed to be so irritatingly slippery and nonintuitive. It took a lot of work to get my mind around these concepts and though I promised myself never to take another semantics and pragmatics course again, I am currently working on exploring this area of linguistics in my dissertation.

I lived at home for the first four years of my undergraduate education. However, my younger sister was just about to graduate from high school and she was quite eager to move out on her own at the earliest possible moment. It amazed her that I was content to live at home at age 22, instead of enjoying the benefits of parental independence. From my point of view, I saw no logical reason to leave home where I felt most comfortable and where I did not have to worry about paying rent and other undesirable expenses. But circumstances soon changed. My mother could no longer afford living in the area where I had lived for most of my life and she made preparations to move to another state. My sister and I found a one-bedroom apartment near the university that was relatively cheap ($700 per month in rent) and we moved in at the beginning of the new academic year. This was a huge change for me. I had a big need for privacy and "alone time," so my sister agreed to sleep in the living room while I got the bedroom; apparently she was just happy to be on her own. The apartment was extremely convenient for me because it was a short walk from the university and grocery store and it was along the main bus lines that could take me anywhere else I wanted. Although we got along okay at first, problems eventually surfaced. I easily got overwhelmed by the accumulation of household goods, mail, clothes, and other assorted objects, and it was a struggle to keep the place from being a complete mess. Then one evening the apartment almost burned down because I had unintentionally left the stove on and absent-mindedly placed a towel over the stove to keep bugs out of the food. This was probably as stupid as unplugging the fire alarm the week before because it had been chirping very irritatingly.

Although the apartment had only one bedroom, my sister decided to invite her best friend and his sister to live with us. I protested to this, but she said she could just as well give me a hundred dollars and have me find my own place to live. Then a few months later her friend's two cousins also stayed for a week. The situation was extremely unpleasant and frustrating even though I still had my bedroom to myself (except when her friends needed clothes from the closet), so I complained to the manager and he told us that we would all be evicted if the illegal subletters remained. Rather quickly the subletters left and several months later, my sister herself moved out to live with her boyfriend. At last I had the apartment all to myself and I liked that very much.

Several years later I completed my M.A. degree and my professors strongly advised me to pursue my Ph.D. at another institution. They said that it would not look good to have all three degrees from the same university. I was not happy to contemplate moving to some other unfamiliar place, and so I did not take the application process very seriously. I applied to only one university and prepared my application materials on the last possible day. This was very similar to how I applied to college after graduating from high school; I had trouble thinking ahead to the future and making preparations to put my life into a new direction. I always wanted things to stay the same way forever, even if things happened to "suck" at the time. But as it turned out, my application was accepted and I was offered a fellowship that was hard to turn down. I realized, too, that the university was the perfect place for me to pursue the studies I was interested in. I had visited the campus earlier in the year and discovered how well suited the program was for me. Some of the professors thought I looked "distracted" when they first met me but that apparently did not figure much in their decision. I had a strong academic record and was the only applicant who had published in the field.

Moving away from my home of many years was a traumatic process, though. I rented a video camera a week before my departure and I videotaped all the places that were familiar to me: the houses where I grew up in, all the schools I attended, various places at the university, the apartment, and so forth. I did not pack most of my belongings until the day before I was supposed to leave and I stayed up the entire night packing. I planned my time so poorly that I had no time to actually clean up the house, and I still had some things left to pack.

My uncle who came to help move my things was very upset at me and I was so broke I had to write a bad check in order to mail my belongings to my new address. Fortunately, I was assigned to live in university housing on campus so I did not have to deal with the stress of trying to find a place to live. But I experienced so much anxiety and stress over the whole event that I had recurring nightmares for three or four months with the same theme: moving day. Each dream had a different setting and involved different people, but the agony was the same.

There was much to like about my new surroundings. The campus was quiet, pretty, and not very crowded. But there was much to get accustomed to and I spent much of my first year somewhat depressed. The social demands at the new university were beyond anything I had yet experienced. There were parties, dinners, and social events in my neighborhood every few weeks. My roommate had friends that would come to the apartment somewhat often. My department would have colloquia, afternoon socials, and parties of their own. I was expected to serve on academic committees and I eventually had teaching responsibilities. These were all new to me.

I have not made many friends here. I think I am generally liked by others but I have not been able to relate well with people here. I am told I come across as shy or even excessively shy and I often have trouble initiating and maintaining social interaction. There are perhaps three or four students here I feel very comfortable speaking with, but I doubt I could consider them friends. I have not done much with any of them outside from departmental functions, aside from attending a few birthday parties. I try to avoid parties because I often leave them feeling very depressed. Sometimes I go to talk and get to know other people in my department, but usually the sole attraction is the food. If there is a lot of commotion and noise, I try to leave before it starts affecting me. When I am with people I do not know or know well, I find it difficult to know what to do. I usually shift into "silent mode" and just watch. I recall one departmental party two years ago that occurred in the midst of a rainstorm. I observed everyone in the room and realized that every single person was engaged in conversation, except me. It turned out this state of affairs lasted almost the entire party. I did not know if I was intentionally being ignored or not, but I remained in the room until every single person had left. Then I went to the blackboard and drew a picture of a woman caught in the rainstorm. The picture seemed to express the discomfort and hurt that I felt and I left it there to be discovered by others.

Aside from the frustration of incidental social contact, I learned that I had difficulties in other areas. Last year I was a member of the organizing committee of an academic conference held at the university and I found it very challenging to participate in group meetings. Topics were discussed too fast for me to think of anything useful to say, people volunteered for duties faster than I could evaluate the work involved, and there were many aspects of the organizing work I knew little or nothing about. I felt very much "out of the loop" and ended up contributing very little. Teaching has also been a challenge. I think I did very well the time I was assigned as a teaching assistant to a course that was squarely within my subspecialty. I felt I knew the material well and I managed to conduct class discussions extemporaneously. The course also largely involved students I knew from my department. But then I was assigned to teach a section of a course that was outside my area of specialization and the section largely included undergraduate students unfamiliar to me. It was not easy. At the end of the course, I received rather negative evaluations from students with comments like "Discussions were awkward and T.A. stuck rather rigidly to list of questions" and "There were HUGE lulls in the discussion and T.A. would not know what to do about them." I also knew the names of only two people out of the dozen students in the section, though I had made a concerted effort to remember whose face went with each name. I think these obstacles may be overcome with a little more teaching experience, as I learn to adapt to these situations.

I think my AS is manifested in fairly subtle ways because I have adapted myself fairly well to the situations I regularly encounter in college life. To most people, I appear to be a shy, quiet, and somewhat awkward person who may sometimes have odd eye gaze, occasionally misunderstand things, and act a little absent-minded now and then. There are a number of things that may appear to be a bit more strange to people who know me better, such as the fact that I made the same thing for dinner for two years (club sandwiches with french fries and a pickle spear, which I liked to eat while listening to the same music every night) or that I like to recite the names of fast food restaurants when they are passed by on the road. The effort I continually make in "appearing ordinary," by suppressing some of my more eccentric tendencies and monitoring what I say and how I interact with others, seems to be overlooked by those who know me. The constant mental perspective-shifting that is required in most social contexts is particularly exhausting to me. I also develop a great deal of anxiety when I interact with others, always wondering if I forgot to say or do something or wondering if the other person thinks I am weird, insensitive, egocentric, or ignorant. I often wish I could set aside these worries and not care what others think, but I seem to be locked into this mindset. At least in my case, anxiety seems to be the price I have to pay for the adaptations I have made.

There are many things that happen almost daily which, while seemingly minor and forgettable, remind me that I often assume different standards than other people and look at the world a little differently. There was the time an old friend visited me when I was living alone and she discovered to her amazement that only one light bulb in the house was working and only then did it dawn on me that I should buy new bulbs. There was the time I complained bitterly to the people at the deli for listing pickles under "condiments" on the menu when in fact a pickle was a vegetable. There was the time I waited outside the departmental secretary's office for an hour and a half because she was on the phone and I thought it would be impolite for me to walk in and sit down (which was what everybody else did in this situation, the secretary later explained to me). There was the time an e-mail penpal of mine went to have cosmetic surgery and I wished her the best in getting her face "butchered up," not realizing I had said anything upsetting. There was the time I stood right up against a stranger at a bus stop in a moment of obliviousness, making him think I was flirting with him when in fact I was hardly aware he was there (as he explained to me, never in his experience has a white woman stood that close to him). I think most of these things could happen to most people, but they seem to happen a lot to me.

On the other hand, as difficult as several aspects of college life have been, I must recognize that AS has been a tremendous advantage to me. In the six years that I researched language use in the past two centuries, I must have looked at hundreds of thousands—if not millions—of pages of text (much of it in manuscript form) in the search for tiny quotations of a specific dialect that hardly anyone bothered to write down. It was truly analogous to the task of searching for a needle in a haystack, and this was work I found immensely enjoyable. Archival research is a tedious, slow, careful process and usually does not yield much data for the time spent. But it is something I do very well and I know few have carried it to the lengths that I have in my field. I doubt I would have gone as far as I have with my research if I wasn't as deeply fascinated with words and so single-minded in my pursuit of research, driven by a need to exhaustively exploit every known archival source. This discipline is highly esteemed in academia, and it is something that comes as naturally to me as, one would imagine, social skills would come to many other people.

I expect my career to continue in academia after I graduate, researching whatever catches my interest and, I would suppose, whatever can be funded in terms of grants. I don't want to think ahead to the next big transition looming in my life, so I won't, but I know it is coming. I would ordinarily hesitate to end this essay without a conclusion but at this point I cannot think of anything that would make a proper ending. This has been one of the most difficult things I have ever had to write and I think I have said enough.

DAWN PRINCE-HUGHES

Dawn is a woman with Asperger's Syndrome. She was diagnosed at age thirty-six by a psychiatrist with prior experience with autism and Asperger's Syndrome, her diagnosis being based on interviews with family and friends and on a thorough examination of her developmental and psychological history. Though her life on the autistic spectrum, like most, has been difficult, her attachment to the ancient past through anthropology has given her context and a sense of belonging. Her work with gorillas taught her how to get along in a world of people she feels are much the same as our distant, ape-like relatives.

Dawn is currently adjunct professor of anthropology at Western Washington University.

I think it is important to start my essay on my university experiences from the beginning. I believe it is important, when looking at the university careers of autistic people, to know how they come to the university—what kind of shape they are in emotionally, developmentally, intellectually, and academically, and how they got that way—in order to better understand them as whole people in the university community. As an anthropologist I might say that personal as well as collective evolution is important to understand.

I remember my own evolution very well. In fact, I remember as far back as being born. People always scoff at the notion that I could possibly have so early a memory, but I also remember once, when I was eight or so, describing the event to my mother who, astounded, con-

firmed my version of what had happened. Some people have speculated, when I have told them, that I had just heard my parents talking
about it and incorporated the information as a personal memory. But,
like most autistic people, I remember details as if a movie were being
played back: the blue/green gowns that the doctor and nurses wore;
the doctor's horn-rim glasses; where my mother's gurney was in the
room; where in the room they took me to dip my tiny feet in ink and
press them onto my birth certificate. It is with this kind of vivid memory that I recall the entirety of my childhood (and the rest of my life,
for that matter) and with this kind of memory that I share my personal
evolution in hopes that it will help other people to embrace the joy
and avoid some of the pain that accompanies living with "the Little
Professor Syndrome" from birth to university and beyond.

My parents were young when they got pregnant, but they were
in love, and they were married. My mother's pregnancy was normal.
After I was born my mother, father, and I all lived with my mother's
parents for a time. It was around this time that I started showing signs
of autism: I disliked being held and did not reach to be picked up. I
could tolerate some cuddling from my grandparents and uncle (who
also lived in the house) because they were quite fat and I liked the way
their bodies felt. It was reassuring somehow.

My developmental milestones were met very early. I skipped crawling and went directly to walking at about eleven months. It wasn't long
after this that I began walking on my tiptoes almost exclusively. This is
sometimes a symptom of autism and happens for two reasons: because
of chronic anxiety, an autistic person's tendons may chronically con-
tract for flight (a very deep physiological response we perhaps inher-
ited as a species from our hunted forebears); and the feel of the ground
may be repellent to an autistic person. I clearly remember learning how
to walk and that both of these factors played a part in my toe-walking.

I talked very early and had an extensive and advanced vocabulary.
I liked and was good at memory games, and I could sing jingles I heard
on television after hearing them only once. I liked acquiring new words

and had a ritual in which I would ride my tricycle up to the dining room table and ask for a new word. One of the adults would give me one, trying to make it too hard for me to say, then I would speed off on my tricycle to follow the circular path from the dining room, to the bathroom, to the living room, and back to the table. On my circular route I would say the word over and over and when I reached the table again I would say the word perfectly and have it memorized for instant recall at any time in the future.

It was about this time that I also developed language idiosyncrasies like using words to describe things as I *sensed* them rather than using the proper word. For example "tang" meant metal, because the sound captured for me how metal tasted and how it felt when it cut. "Bang-bow" described the action of the light switch. I talked incessantly, earning myself the nickname "Jabberbox." I could duplicate accents and repeat pieces of dialogue exactly. I would, while avoiding eye contact with my captive audiences, perform long monologues. My periods of monologue were broken up frequently by periods when I wouldn't listen to or respond to people. However, loud or unusual sounds would affect me far more profoundly than other children and I would be very upset by them. Also at this time I began to take phrases literally. When my mother told me that a road sign (I always wanted to know what signs said) declared "Pass with Care," I believed we were breaking the law because we didn't have a nurse in the car with us. It also started to be important to me at this time to take the same routes without deviation when we went somewhere.

As I got older, around four or five, I started to have fascinations with objects: kitchen utensils, rocks, tools. I liked to watch tools and gadgets work over and over. Mixers and wrenches were great. I delighted in watching my grandparents use these things and perform the same motions over and over. I remember feeling like these tools and devices had *meaning* and *perfection*. Other objects, such as marionettes, mannequins, and dolls, terrified me.

I wanted to know how things worked and I would take them apart. Nothing was off-limits to me; I would dismantle phones, paper fans, toys, small engines, seed packets, and hearing aids. My parents misunderstood and thought I was destructive at times. Though I had no regard for the possessions of others, I felt intense attachments to my own things: my tinker toys, my rock and bone collection, my stuffed animals, all would be meticulously arranged and guarded. Woe to anyone who moved any part of an arrangement. I felt terrible anxiety when things were moved or changed.

I felt the same way about my clothing. I had favorite articles of clothing, usually soft, cotton, and a size too large, that I would not take off because it took a couple of days of wearing for my clothes to feel right. My mother used to have to take them off me at night to wash them. I stuck to my favorite clothes and dressed inappropriately for the weather; I wore coats I liked in the summer and would go without socks (and shoes if I could get away with it) in the winter.

In other sensory areas I also displayed oddities. I was addicted to certain smells. I would stick my nose in the Band-aid box and breathe deeply until someone made me stop. I felt the same way about my grandparents' denture cleanser, autumn leaves, tomato plants, my grandmother's purse, and the worm bin my grandfather kept in the basement. I made the adults in my life play certain records over and over and over again while I windmilled my right arm vigorously. I used to get up and wander around the house at night because it was dark and didn't hurt my eyes.

This brings to mind another autistic trait: love of specific place. I loved my grandparents' house as one would love the dearest and closest of relatives. I can still draw a complete floor plan of that house and describe in detail what was in every cabinet and drawer. I can also complete this exercise for the second house I lived in and all four public schools I attended. This ability to remember my schools did not stem from love but rather from survival instincts.

Kindergarten

The day I had to leave my mother and go into the kindergarten building is among the worst memories of my life. I felt lost and bewildered. The loud children, the bright fluorescent lights, the strange smells and hard desks and chairs made me want to run away and hide. These elements of school were not to change throughout my entire public school career and I never got used to them. I remember standing outside the entryway door to the building, stiff with dread and confusion. The only thing I could think to do was to pick up a pebble and run back to give it to my mother, a representative of myself that she could keep safe. This was the first time I got in trouble at school (we were supposed to be lining up single-file to enter the building, and I broke out of line to run to my mother). It was in many ways downhill from there.

My teacher wanted to send me home because I knew all the material and I was disruptive in class, as I wanted to do things that were more fun than the teacher's planned activities. This, coupled with the fact that I had no respect for her authority, made for a good many run-ins. Luckily for me the teacher actually liked me a lot and thought I was very bright and that this was the problem. My parents opted to keep me in kindergarten, hoping I would do better with time. What happened was that I became withdrawn and fearful of breaking rules. I became very serious and kept my learning interests private. I detached from my classes and lived completely in my own fantasy world.

Elementary School

In first grade I became increasingly obsessed with rules. I studied people's behavior and actions and read written rules carefully to try to make sense of my school community and fellow human beings. Often what they said or recorded as the rules were, in fact, not standard human practice. I began policing the playground to make sure students did not break the rules: that they didn't fight, didn't swear, didn't take things from each other, that they didn't call each other names. I was very much concerned with morality and remember talking to my grandparents' pastor about right and wrong and the nature of sin. I would cite moral reasons that my playground backsliders should cease and desist in their nefarious undertakings. Needless to say, this did not go over well with my peers. They made it clear that I should go away.

I ended up standing with the teachers throughout recess and would join in their conversations. I would always try to bring the subject around to religion, politics, and the roots of human nature. I realized I felt more comfortable with them. Once I came to this realization, I tried to stick with adult company and did not, after that point, have any enduring peer friendships to speak of.

By third grade I was thoroughly disgusted with human behavior (what I understood of it, and I was understanding less as time went on). The loud bells, the smell of institutional cleaners, the rowdiness of my peers, the screech of chalk on the board, and a growing disparity in my academic abilities were starting to take a toll. I became depressed and began to speak in monotone and never smile. I developed asthma.

My third-grade teacher was from the old school and believed my problem was willfulness and heaped extra work on me. I remember I was terrible at math so she would send piles of math homework home with me. I would just sit and stare at it and go numb. She would scream at me in class and I would dissociate, totally leave my body, and I was literally unable to see my surroundings. She would force me to look at her by clutching my face with both hands. The memory still makes me feel sick. I would go home, go down to the basement, and hide in the tiny space between the wall and the furnace and listen to its perfect mechanical pulsing. I would soak up its heat and symmetry.

After the first part of third grade I began to spend all my free time in the forest next to our house. There was a little stream that ran through it, and a wonderful underpass which our country road passed over. I would stand inside it, where the water ran through, and beat on the walls with stones for hours. I loved the echo and the repetition. It was also dark and hidden and safe.

I pretended to be a forest ranger and would clean up the trash people threw from the road and clear debris from the stream. I started a crawdad breeding project where I kept eggs in a bucket until they hatched, protecting them from predators. I would look at the eggs and hatchlings under my father's microscope to make sure they were healthy. I would do this also with stream water to make sure it was free of pollution. I grew very attached to that small island of land.

I think it was during the beginning of fourth grade that we were allowed to take time out from regular class to work on a project. My mother bought me a several-piece model of a Neandertal man to put together at school. Well, that was it. Human evolution and the origins of behavior became my consuming passions and continued from that time on to be the dominant forces in my life.

I scrapped the ranger idea, convinced that rangers were just representatives of the wicked taming force of recent civilization. I became "David of the Jungle." I made spears and constructed my own shelters from leaves and branches. I made tools with stones and collected edible plants from the woods. I dug in the streambed looking for fossils. I took my shirt off and wore primitive beads.

In fifth grade I had a wonderful teacher, who introduced me to creative writing as a means of expressing myself. She cut out nearly all of the math in my program and focused on my strengths: English, social studies, and reading. She allowed me to edit a class poetry newsletter. She would talk to me for as long as I wanted about the subjects that were meaningful to me. I remember sitting in the woods (sans shirt, plus beads) writing and writing about everything and anything that took my fancy. I felt free.

Unfortunately, the same beloved woods that nurtured my soul and my intellect were tough on my body. I was allergic to most of the plants there, as well as mold (which in Southern Illinois is appreciable) and our cats, who came to keep me company when I was in the woods. The doctors strongly suggested we move out west.

My parents sold everything, and my sister and I were told to give most of our things away as we prepared to go west with nothing but our VW camper, destination unknown. The age of ten years is difficult for everyone, worse for people with autism. Moving at that age, in addition to giving up house, home, grandparents, and almost all possessions to go somewhere completely undecided, is enough to destroy an autistic person. About this time I began "stealing" personal items from people I loved. Looking back it is clear that I needed connection and control, and keeping a belonging of someone I loved close to me gave me those things. I never stole anything from stores, the way some kids experiment. Regardless of my moral justifications in hindsight, my parents really started to worry about me at this time. Unfortunately, things got much worse before they got better.

Middle School and High School

Looking back, I think I had what can be described as a complete coming apart after our move to Montana. I abandoned my focus on nature and the evolution of humankind for a more (or at least I thought so at the time) appropriate preoccupation: I was an alien from outer space. It solved so many problems and explained so much about me, both to myself and to my peers. Actually, it did not serve to explain anything to my peers except that I was crazy and to be avoided at best, beaten up at worst.

My schoolwork went to hell. I didn't care about anything anymore. The schools were terrible in terms of curriculum and diversity and were designed only to give future ranchers and loggers the most basic of educations. I read Shakespeare and D. H. Lawrence and prayed for my *real* people to come and get me in a flying saucer and take me home where I would no longer be laughed at, sensorily assaulted, confused and awkward, and odd. They, of course, never came.

As a result I went back to my familiar fascination with all things archaic and evolving. I retreated to the forest once more and there was a lot of it to retreat to. The tiny town where we lived was surrounded by true wilderness. I wandered for hours with my literature and field guides, works on Indians and wilderness survival. Occasionally I had a side interest, like playing the drums or harmonica, but if I wasn't good at something immediately, I quit. "Practice" was not an idea that held sway with me, so I would return with full force and renewed vigor to my core interest.

In my eighth-grade year, ideas about evolution of material culture and behavioral evolution led me to the study of philosophy, which I soon believed was essential to the field of anthropology. I read Plato and Locke and my favorite was Kant. His discourses on morality were easy to follow and informed my view of the world and my behavior. I decided, based on my understanding of the Kantian model of morality, that it was wrong not to divulge any secret, any thought about oneself or about the world at any time.

I entered my freshman year of high school with this conviction. There were things I said and did, things I divulged, that most high schoolers would rather die than do or say. I was utterly ostracized. By that point I didn't care what anyone thought of me as long as I was acting in accordance with my beliefs. I buried myself in my studies, which were far ahead of anything anyone else in school was doing, while I quietly failed in all my classes. I didn't see anyone when I walked down the halls. Just as in third grade, I literally didn't see them. Between being physically assaulted for being who I was and flunking out so dismally, I decided to quit school.

I left, got my GED, though I was only a sophomore when I quit, and determined that I would never step foot in a classroom again.

College

I lost several years after I left home. I was homeless and without job skills and certainly without people skills. I was so shell-shocked that just the thought of trying to find the Employment Security Office made me feel like hiding. I survived through the help of kind people, many of them strangers, and slept in stairwells and ate from garbage cans when I was forced to.

Difficulty orientating in space and finding one's way around is a symptom of autism. When I did try to get out of my situation, gathered up all my courage and went to seek employment, my lack of eye contact, strange speech patterns, and obvious lack of marketable skills made finding work impossible.

I found people—artists, singers, activists, and other *avant garde* as strange as (or stranger than) me—who ignored or cherished my differences. Though some people took advantage of my social shortcomings and naiveté, there were many generous people who took me in, believed in me, and helped me get on the right road. The road that I had always been best suited for but had been kept from by a rotten school system: higher academics. I knew I could not cope sensorily with traditional college at that point in my life. I was just finding my educational footing again. I found an animal sciences program that allowed me to work externally in approved mentoring situations. While I completed coursework I also trained under private practice vets specializing in exotic animals as well as under vets and technicians at a local zoo. I studied animal behavior as well. I eventually was assigned to observe gorillas during a particular gorilla's illness. The gorillas took to me, and I did so well that the director of research at the zoo met with me and asked me about my plans for the future. I remember him reading over my observation notes and chuckling to himself with an enigmatic smile, saying, "This is very good. Yes, very, very good . . ." (only later did I realize what a magnificent compliment this was). I told him about the program I was currently enrolled in and my interest in human evolution. I told him that when the two-year program was over I would like to pursue a B.A. in anthropology. I didn't know at that time that I had a form of autism, but I knew I wasn't equipped to go through the traditional protocol of regular college. I was pathologically sensitive to intellectual and academic criticism, my skills in math and linear processes continued to be uneven, I didn't understand my peers. I still had distracting nervous tics. And something as simple as trying to navigate my way through a campus would be very difficult, and take my energy away from learning. I was also prosopagnostic, meaning I couldn't easily tell people apart.

The director of research told me that with my intelligence I would

certainly be able to study on my own, with some guidance. He agreed
to sponsor a series of gorilla behavior research projects that I did in fact
use toward my undergraduate degree. Though the combined B.A./
M.A. program I enrolled in allowed me to work externally, and accepted
my two-year animal behavior program and gorilla studies toward my
requirements for graduation, I was forced to take several years of anthropology courses in a classroom setting as well. At first I dreaded
this. And, sure enough, the sensory problems remained. However,
when I realized I already knew everything being taught from my previous private studying, I was able to relax. I have heard that it is difficult for autistic people to learn face-to-face because of the discomfort
they experience from the physical proximity of the teacher. This is
certainly true of me. I was lucky that I didn't need to learn anything, I
just had to be pleasant and considerate of people, which was becoming easier as I studied and spent time with the gorillas.

I was learning a lot about myself as I studied and learned about
wild and captive primate behavior. I knew what a captive primate felt
like when it rocked and paced its too small cage. Some people have
speculated that primates evince autistic-like behavior because they
don't get enough stimulation. While I am a strong supporter of en-
riched and enlarged captive habitats, I think that the reason primates
(and other animals) act this way is because they cannot control or
escape the stimuli they are bombarded with. Huge, staring crowds, all
noisy and smelly, the unpleasant tactile experience of concrete and the
visual offense of bars all combine to make them go nuts. I really em-
pathize with the way they must feel. That kind of chronic anxiety is
devastating.

Though their research is never cited anymore, I agree with Elisabeth and Niko Tinbergen in regard to their work *Autistic Children: New
Hope for a Cure* (1983). They believe that modern life with its unnatural
living conditions, chemicals, broken-down social systems, and chronic
stress overstimulate and assault the human animal, causing some to
manifest the biological and psychological matrix we call autism. They

charge that as animals, we engage in all kinds of behaviors that, in autistic people, become tight feedback loops almost impossible to get out of: conflicted approach and avoidance rituals, motivational conflicts, inhibited intention movements, displacement activities. Zoo animals do all these things. I often felt like exactly that myself: an anxious animal in a zoo.

I am blessed to have found a place to escape that chronic anxiety. The gorillas had an enormously calming effect on me. They knew and recognized me, briefly acknowledging my presence each time I sat with them. But their behavior was subtle. They hardly ever looked at me. They would sit near me with their eyes averted. Staring—like normal people in our culture consider polite in conversation—is rude and threatening to nonhuman primates. Their social subtleties and calm demeanor allowed me to relax and really watch what they were doing. I saw social *cause and effect* for the first time. When I realized that their behavior was so much like human behavior I knew I would learn everything I needed to know from them.

I began to cautiously apply the things I'd learned from the gorillas —how to put people at ease by sitting near them and acknowledging them with a quick glance and smile ("smiles" evolved from submissive primate grimaces and mean that a person intends no harm), how to avoid arguments by putting your hands up and head down—and I began to have some success. I actually made some friends. They affectionately dubbed me "The All-Knowing Piece of Shit." Though this doesn't sound very affectionate, it was. They smiled and shoved me when they said it.

It was during this time that I had an extensive series of cognitive and skill tests, as it was clear to my college instructors that I had some kind of disability, which showed up in my uneven skills. My IQ test revealed very superior scores in many areas and very low scores in some others. My verbal, memory, and comprehension test scores were extremely good, while anything involving numbers was pretty dismal. While I reached test ceilings in my strong areas, I had what equaled a fourth-grade level of skill and comprehension in mathematics. My IQ, scattered abilities aside, was in the very top percentage of the population. This kind of pattern is common in autism. Other autistic markers were recorded at that time: odd prosody, unusual approaches to problem solving and unconventional thinking styles, a disregard for convention in dress and hairstyle, and some neurological problems. Still no one realized I had an Autism Spectrum Disorder, and the college was uncertain as to how to really help me.

Yet, all in all, my college experience was good. As I moved forward to the M.A. portion of my program, I enjoyed working on my thesis and beginning to become involved with my colleagues in the field. I actually became known as an achiever, if an odd one. My thesis was interdisciplinary, a trend that is only now gaining some acceptance, and at conferences I enjoyed debating esoteric connections between anthropology, psychology, and physics. I wrote and presented papers on gorillas at regional anthropology conferences and at sponsored conferences of the Jane Goodall Institute. I started to become aware that I could talk to people very well and even become very enthusiastic about interacting socially if it revolved around my areas of interest. The dean of the college in which I received my undergraduate classroom credits met with me to congratulate me on my accomplishments and suggested we have lunch sometime. I don't know if he thought it was weird that I paid more attention to the interesting lamp on his desk than I did to him.

Graduate School

As my M.A. program drew to a close, I knew I wanted to pursue a Ph.D. Though at the time it was only for myself—I didn't think anyone would ever accept me as a full-fledged Ph.D.—my love of learning and the exploration of ideas had been reawakened, and people in my field were getting to know me, like me, and respect and admire my work. Though my academic career had been vastly different than that of anyone else I knew (and at times I was self-conscious about this), people were intrigued by and envious of the fact that I worked alone under the direction of mentors. People would say, "Oh! I wish I had been able to work like you! When I think back on my college and university days, all I can remember is crippling anxiety and constant panic. I would have gone so much further in my thinking if I had been allowed to." Now that I know that there are other career academics who have autism spectrum disorders I often wonder how many of my colleagues would have benefited from programs like mine.

I literally searched the world for a doctoral program that would permit me to continue to work in the solitary manner which had brought me so far. I quickly learned that Europe was far ahead of the United States in terms of an openness to progressive ideas and a long tradition of mentoring over coursework as we think of it here. Upon this discovery I narrowed my search to Northern Europe.

My research with gorillas and fascination with the "core ideas" or archetypes that shape emergent culture and that bind us to our ancient past and earlier ways of being and perceiving led me to search the home of archetypal research: Switzerland. I did, indeed, find a university that fit my criteria. My application was successful, though because their standards were more stringent, they did not fully accept my previous degrees; I would have to test into their program and rewrite my M.A. thesis before beginning their doctoral program.

I traveled to Switzerland, where I spent a day at the university completing oral exams, providing and explaining the documentation of my undergraduate studies, exhaustively relating the methods and findings of my previous research, and defending my new thesis and its weak points. When this was finished, I defended my dissertation proposal. Obviously, it was exhausting; especially because I hadn't slept in twenty-four hours. I found the actual grilling at the university exhilarating, as I love to talk about my work and ideas. It was the travel that was hard for me. This is true of most autistic people, who don't take change well. You can imagine the stress of a different country with a different language. I had been unable to sleep on the plane over, then I had to find and wait for a series of trains to the university.

After I passed examinations, chose my advisors in the States, and had my dissertation focus approved, I worked on my dissertation for the next several years. I completed my defense with the university's highest marks.

Life

After I finished my degree I jumped into teaching and lecturing wherever I could find an opportunity to do so. Many occasions presented themselves for me to guest lecture, present at conferences, or to offer series of topical workshops or talks. Though I applied to several universities, however, I was unable to find a tenure-track position.

This is the situation autistic people often find themselves in. This can occur for several reasons, including poor interview skills due to anxiety (I had one interview, and it didn't go very well), the inability to select and prioritize pertinent information on a written application, and an aversion to the social situations that jobs present. In my case, I think my alternative education was the first hurdle. As I said, it is only now that job candidates with interdisciplinary degrees are being accepted and even sought out. Secondly, though I can choose and prioritize any material I teach without any problem at all, it is difficult for me to know for certain what a search committee is looking for. There are many unwritten rules in writing an application and the requisite cover letter. An autistic person will think to herself, "Well, it's clear from my vita that I'm qualified and how I got that way. They probably would want to know more about who I am, since we will have to work together for many years if I'm hired." Based on this line of thinking, the autistic applicant will complete a very personal (and inappropriate) cover letter. Because of this the applicant won't make it past the first screening. Another thing I used to do was send work in its early stages, sometimes even preliminary notes, to potential employers and colleagues in order to share my projects with them. My reasoning was that if I respected and admired someone, I would want her or his input at the barest beginning of a project so that we could discuss every facet of it *as a process together*. It was my way of trying to really connect with people I liked. I thought such sharing would give hiring committees insight into how I thought. I believed it would be fun to talk about the foundations of my projects with interviewing teams. Now I realize that most people feel this is unprofessional, and no matter how much you respect and admire someone, you must present them only with finished and unassailable pieces of work. That makes me sad somehow as it seems like a very self-centered way to create.

Though I was getting lots of temporary work, often with honoraria, it was becoming clear to me that I was not going to be hired anywhere. With my dissertation finished and the safety of the degree program behind me, I felt lost and depressed. I was doing very well with people, but I started doing the thing that always gets autistic people in trouble: I was starting to try to pass as totally normal. I became more anxious as I worked hard to follow every conversation and respond appropriately, do things the way everyone else did them, and try to care about the things everyone else seemed to. As I worked harder and got more discouraged I grew more panicked. I got angry easily and often felt like I was dying. Later I learned these were panic attacks. By this time I had a partner and a son and they did not enjoy being around this kind of tension. My partner almost left me. Something had to be done. I began reading about my symptoms and eventually found a good book on Asperger's Syndrome. I went to a psychologist who knew about the dis/order.

I was diagnosed with Asperger's Syndrome when I was thirty-six years old. Suddenly my entire life made sense. I felt an overwhelming sense of relief. Armed with an understanding of what made me the way I am, I have been able to relax and teach myself how better to get along. I changed my diet and began taking medication. I can now explain my behavior to others and put them at ease.

As a result of my discovery and the resulting changes in my life I've been able to make many new friends and keep them. I was able to get an appointment at the university in my town. My family life is good and I am very close to my son. I feel that my life is perfect and that I am perfectly fine the way I am.

My heart goes out to people like me, perhaps much younger and just starting out in academia. They know they are different from other people. They don't know why. They only know that learning is keeping them alive. I dedicate this essay to them in the hope that they will survive, that they find it and read it, and get help. And I hope that someday, with less pain, they, too, feel that their life is perfect and that they are perfectly fine the way they are.

A Compendium for
the Inclusive University

Common Challenges for Autistic Students
and What Universities Can Do about Them

Below is a list of common challenges that university students with
autism have mentioned in their essays and in personal communications.
The responses suggested here are inexpensive and simple. Counselors,
faculty, or staff members should use the following list of issues and
solutions as a guide only. They should work closely with their autistic
students to determine each student's *unique* needs and respond to challenges with the student's input.

Misdiagnosis:

People with autism are often misdiagnosed with disorders or conditions
that are only a potential part of Autistic Spectrum Disorder: Tourette's
Syndrome, epilepsy, Obsessive/Compulsive Disorder, Generalized
Anxiety Disorder, ADHD, and Anorexia Nervosa. It is important for
university counselors to learn about autism and its manifestations. A
correct diagnosis of autism profoundly affects approaches to treatment
and medication.

Psychological counseling:

University counselors should be aware that talk therapy does not work
for treatment of autism. Also, medications should be tested at low

doses, as autistic people are often sensitive to medications and will respond to low doses. Counseling should revolve around helping autistic students cope with life *as they are*. It should not focus on changing the autistic person, though attention to adaptive stategies will be useful, as advised and illustrated in several of these essays.

Academic advising:

Autistic students may not be able to cope with a full course load. Advisors should keep a student's potential limitations in mind. Breaks lasting a full quarter or semester may be needed. A secondary issue, autistic students' frequent reluctance to study subjects outside their areas of special interest, can be remedied by finding classes that link different subjects together. Also, an advisor should help the student give early consideration to his or her ultimate career goals.

Career counseling:

Help autistic students learn basics. Teach them how to fill out an application and write a cover letter, how to dress for and what to do in an interview. What might seem obvious to you may not be to the student you are helping.

Learning styles:

Students may have scattered abilities. Early testing can help students and faculty, as well as advisors, determine the best educational approach for the student. Some students will need tutors in their weak areas. Some students learn better moving from complex to simple rather than vice versa. Some will have a hard time discerning pertinent information in lectures. Handouts can help.

Testing:

Students might need a longer period to finish tests. Being left alone in a separate room is also a strategy that works well. Instructions should be very clear and may need to be repeated. If sample tests are given, they should be identical in organization to the test. Extra time should be allowed for projects, as autistic students will often get "hooked" on them. They may need help narrowing topics and organizing information.

Social challenges:

Clubs that focus on the autistic student's areas of interest can help him or her meet people. Chess club, physics club, anthropology club—all these types of gatherings provide ready topics for students to open up with. Also, autistic students will often do better interacting with faculty in their area of interest. Inclusion can be well worth the effort. However, some autistic students may not *want* social interaction. This should be respected.

Need for sameness:

Students may need to sit in the same place in class each day. They may need to carry "odd" objects to class and around campus with them. This is a way to feel anchored and should not be discouraged. Changing classes may be very difficult for students with autism. The use of a personal guide can help. Advisors may consider helping the student choose classes that are held in the same room or in the same building. Taping a campus map to the back of a notebook is another solution.

Housing:

Most autistic students find it difficult if not impossible to live with others. Dorm living may work if the student has a private room. Rentals with roommates are usually not an option. Some students do better if they can continue to live with parents. People diagnosed with autism are eligible for social services, including housing assistance and social security payments that can help with rent.

Daily maintenance:

Students may need help organizing daily activities, paying bills on time, and maintaining bank accounts. In addition, keeping assignments and class schedules straight is obviously important. Shopping for essentials can be accomplished with the help of an aide.

Diversity issues:

It is easy to forget that autistic people come from different ethnic groups, struggle with gender issues, and have different sexual orientations. These realities further accent the struggles of autistic students. Diversity counselors and liaisons should learn about autism and consider it in their outreach and diversity workshops.

Prosopagnosia:

Many autistic people have problems recognizing faces, even those of people they have met many times. Sometimes the problem is only contextual, but for some students this will be a constant challenge. Students may not be able to distinguish a professor from a classmate. Name tags in class may be a solution. Outside of class, people approaching the autistic student should let the student know who they are and where they have met before.

"Disruptive" behavior:

Rocking, coughing, and grimacing are examples of the many tic behaviors that autistic people use in order to calm down and focus. Often such behaviors distract or irritate classmates. Professors may interpret these behaviors as signs that a student is not paying attention when quite the opposite is true. It should be explained to everyone affected that this behavior is necessary for the autistic student to be able to focus.

Sensory problems:

Touch:

The feel of fixed desks and chairs: Allow the student to use a comfortable chair, brought from home or chosen from an on-campus lounge. Allow the student to choose where the chair will be placed each day.

The feel of clothing: Many autistic people need to wear baggy cotton clothing, giving them a "rumpled" appearance. Trying to encourage them to wear better-fitting clothing is a mistake. If they are uncomfortable in their clothes, they will be unable to concentrate.

The feel of water: Some autistic people are overwhelmed by showers. If a student begins to smell bad, tell him or her. Help the student set up a schedule and method of bathing that works for the individual. Hair washing and styling are other problems. Some autistic people have very touchy scalps. Help them find a stylist they like who will listen to them and work with their needs. If they don't care about their appearance, respect that.

The feel of chalk: Let students use an overhead projector or computer and video projector to illustrate their ideas.

Sound:

Listening to lectures: Many autistic people have trouble screening out background noise. They can't listen and take notes at the same time. Handouts with notes on the lecture would help. Insist on quiet during lectures. Also, schedule breaks and provide a quiet place out of the class where the student can rest.

General campus noise: Earplugs work well for many autistic people.

Sight:

Tunnel vision: Under stress, many students experience this phenomenon. Cutting down on the general stimulation level of the room (lights, noise) can help.

Light sensitivity: Fluorescent lights can be a problem. Dark glasses or tinted lenses can help. Some students find a personal desk light helps.

Color sensitivity: See *Light sensitivity.*

Smell:

Some autistic students are very sensitive to odors. Ask other students in the class to avoid using cologne and perfume. Don't use dry-erase markers or industrial cleaners.

Taste:

Some autistic people are very picky eaters. This is often because of sensitivities to the flavor or texture of particular foods. Students will often eat one item almost exclusively. It is a good idea for the cafeteria to stock plenty of this item.

Notes

Preface

1. Francesca G. E. Happé, "The Autobiographical Writings of Three Asperger Syndrome Adults: Problems of Interpretation and Implications for Theory," in *Autism and Asperger Syndrome*, ed. Uta Frith, 207–42 (Cambridge: Cambridge University Press, 1991).

Introduction

1. *Diagnostic and Statistical Manual of Mental Disorders*, 4th ed. (Washington, D.C.: American Psychiatric Association, 1994), 70–71.

2. Some people with Asperger's have written about their experiences; the reader can consult the bibliography of this work to locate books by Temple Grandin and Donna Williams. Also, an interesting paper on the personal reportage of persons with Asperger's Syndrome is Francesca G. E. Happé's "The Autobiographical Writings of Three Asperger Syndrome Adults: Problems of Interpretation and Implications for Theory," in *Autism and Asperger Syndrome*, ed. Uta Frith, 207–42 (Cambridge: Cambridge University Press, 1991).

3. Lawrence Osborn, "The Little Professor Syndrome," *New York Times Magazine*, 18 June 2000, 55–61.

4. There is still debate about what criteria should be used to fix certain points on the autism spectrum. For the most part, the essayists in this anthology believe that as individuals, we will never show identical clinical pictures and that all of our "symptoms" and personality traits scatter differently.

5. Since Hans Asperger's time and with a broadening of diagnostic criteria it is now estimated that the ratio of boys to girls with Asperger's Syndrome is 3:1. Many girls and women with Asperger's may go undiagnosed, as they are more likely to get intensive social training and may manifest fewer serious social

problems, such as aggression, due to female biology. Interestingly, most of the contributors to this anthology are female.

6. Uta Frith, "Asperger and His Syndrome," in *Autism and Asperger Syndrome*, ed. Uta Frith, 1–36.

7. American Psychiatric Association, *Diagnostic and Statistical Manual*, 4th ed., 77.

8. Dr. Margaret L. Bauman, a neurologist at Harvard Medical School, for example, believes autism can be traced back to the middle of the second trimester of pregnancy, while Dr. Patricia M. Rodier, an embryologist at the University of Rochester School of Medicine, believes that the origins of autism occur between the twentieth and twenty-fourth days of gestation. Others, including Dr. Eric Courchesne, neuroscientist at the University of California, San Diego, posits that autism could just as easily develop after birth. In terms of causes, Bruno Bettelheim has claimed that "blame" for autism can be laid squarely at the doorstep of cold and unresponsive mothers (a theory very much out of fashion today), while more current researchers believe that autism is a wholly organic phenomenon.

9. See David Weeks and Jamie James's *Eccentrics: A Study of Sanity and Strangeness* (New York: Random House, 1995).

Darius

1. As sign-language doesn't have sounds, verbal rhyme cannot exist. I wondered whether it would be possible to have visual rhyme or alliteration. And how about the rhythm of the hand movements—could there be a visual type of metrics? Perhaps visual poetry might have more in common with dance?

2. At that time I had forgotten that I was gay myself. I realized this when I was younger, though I didn't have a word for it then. When I was eleven I read books by a famous homosexual author, who was very graphic in his descriptions. I immediately identified with him, but somehow this did not lead to explicit identification with being gay.

3. Previously, I simply attributed my lack of recognition to a general bad memory.

4. Recently I found out that though I do not recognize people when I meet them and am likely to confuse them with someone else who has the same general characteristics, I do have an accurate picture of them in my mind. When I compare those pictures, I can see that those two people are not at all alike. In other words, when I see Caroline I may not recognize her, or mistakenly perceive her as Marian, but when I scan their respective images in my mind, I can

see that Caroline and Marian are not at all alike, apart from basic visuals (height, color of the hair, etc.). I have painted several portraits of people by heart and these are always recognized by other people as good portraits. Face-blindness may have several different possible causes. There are also people who are able to recognize people, but cannot hold an accurate representation of their faces in their mind.

5. I may not recognize someone, but I often know that I should. I have become quite expert at faking recognition.

6. One of the funnier context-effects is the effect alcohol has on me. I can drink quite a lot of alcohol in surroundings where I normally also drink alcohol. If I go to a bar I have never been to before, I become intoxicated on even one glass of wine. NTs do not experience this kind of reaction to the same extent (though there is something similar, especially in heroin users. This is the reason that so many addicts die abroad. The same dose affects them in a much bigger way in a foreign environment).

7. Paraphrase of Maslow's perceptive and cutting remark about "normality" being mistakenly seen as the height of mental health.

8. NB: this is true the other way around as well! NT-autism researchers would do well to be more aware of their own NT-bias. Talk of theory of mind skills. . . .

9. The capacity to know that other people have a mind in which they have thoughts and feelings that may not be the same as the ones we are currently experiencing.

Bibliography

Online Resources

(Note: World Wide Web sites and e-mail addresses are current as of the date of publication.)

E-mail groups for university students with autism:

owner-autuniv-l@lists.dircon.co.uk

AS-and-Proud-of-it@yahoogroups.com

Autism and Asperger's Syndrome web pages:

Online Asperger Syndrome Information and Support (O.A.S.I.S.):

  http://www.udel.edu/bkirby/asperger/

Autism Society of America:

  http://www.autism-society.org

The National Autistic Society (NAS)/UK:

  http://www.nas.org.uk

Web site maintained by people with autism/Asperger's Syndrome:

  http://www.amug.org/~a203/

Ooops . . . Wrong Planet! Syndrome:

  http://www.isn.net/~jypsy/

Works Cited

American Psychiatric Association. *Diagnostic and Statistical Manual of Mental Disorders.* 4th ed. Washington, D.C.: American Psychiatric Association, 1994.

Attwood, Tony. *Asperger's Syndrome: A Guide for Parents and Professionals.* London: Jessica Kingsley Publishers, 1998.

Eisenmajer, Richard, and Margot Prior. "Comparison of Symptoms in Autism and Asperger's Disorder." *Journal of the American Academy of Child and Adolescent Psychiatry* 35 (1996): 1523–32.

Fisman, S., M. Steele, J. Short, T. Byrne, and C. Lavallee. "Case Study: Anorexia Nervosa and Autistic Disorder in an Adolescent Girl." *Journal of the American Academy of Child and Adolescent Psychiatry* 35 (1996): 937–40.

Frith, Uta. "Asperger and His Syndrome." In *Autism and Asperger Syndrome,* ed. Uta Frith. Cambridge: Cambridge University Press, 1991.

Gillberg, C. "Autism and Anorexia Nervosa: Related Conditions?" *Nordisk Psykiatrisk Tidsskrift* 39 (1985): 307–12.

Grandin, Temple. *Thinking in Pictures: And Other Reports from My Life with Autism.* New York: Doubleday, 1995.

Grandin, Temple, and Margaret M. Scariano. *Emergence, Labeled Autistic.* Tunbridge Wells: Costello, 1986.

Happé, Francesca G. E. "The Autobiographical Writings of Three Asperger Syndrome Adults: Problems of Interpretation and Implications for Theory." In *Autism and Asperger Syndrome,* ed. Uta Frith. Cambridge: Cambridge University Press, 1991.

Miedzianik, David. *My Autobiography.* Nottingham: Child Development Research Unit, University of Nottingham, 1986.

Osborn, Lawrence. "The Little Professor Syndrome." *New York Times Magazine,* 18 June 2000, 55–61.

Schneider, Edgar. *Discovering My Autism: Apologia Pro Vita Sua* (with Apologies to Cardinal Newman). London: Jessica Kingsley Publishers, 1998.

Susman, Edward. "How to Tell Asperger's from Autism." *Brown University Child and Adolescent Behavior Letter* 1 (1996): 1–3.

Tantam, Digby. "Eccentricity and Autism." Ph.D. thesis, University of London.

Tinbergen, Niko, and Elisabeth A. Tinbergen. *Autistic Children: New Hope for a Cure.* London: George Allen and Unwin, 1983.

Weeks, David, and Jamie James. *Eccentrics: A Study of Sanity and Strangeness.* New York: Random House, 1995.

Williams, Donna. *Autism and Sensing: The Unlost Instinct.* London: Jessica Kingsley Publishers, 1998.

———. *Nobody Nowhere: The Extraordinary Autobiography of an Autistic.* London: Transworld Publishers, 1992.

———. *Somebody Somewhere: Breaking Free from the World of Autism.* London: Transworld Publishers, 1994.

Williams, Karen. "Understanding the Student with Asperger's Syndrome: Guidelines for Teachers." *Focus on Autistic Behavior* 10 (1995): 9–17.